The HAUNTING *of* LOUISIANA

The
HAUNTING
of
LOUISIANA

Barbara Sillery

**Photographs by
Oak Lea and Danielle Genter**

Foreword by Phillip J. Jones

PELICAN PUBLISHING COMPANY
Gretna 2003

*The word "Pelican" and the depiction of a pelican are trademarks
of Pelican Publishing Company, Inc., and are registered
in the U.S. Patent and Trademark Office.*

Library of Congress Cataloging-in-Publication Data

Sillery, Barbara.
   The haunting of Louisiana / Barbara Sillery ; photographs
by Oak Lea and Danielle Genter ; foreword by Phillip J.
Jones.
     p. cm.
  Includes bibliographical references (p.).
  ISBN 1-56554-905-8 (pbk.)
  1. Ghosts—Louisiana. I. Title.

BF1472.U6 S55 2001
133.1'09763—dc21

                                2001036193

*All photographs by Oak Lea except chapter 20, epilogue, and author
photographs by Danielle Genter*

Printed in the United States of America
Published by Pelican Publishing Company, Inc.
1000 Burmaster Street, Gretna, Louisiana 70053

To my three muses:
Danielle Dawn
Rebecca Aimée
Heather ("Tinker Bell") Anne

Contents

Foreword

I am delighted to have appeared in Barbara Sillery's documentary, *The Haunting of Louisiana*. It was a pleasure to get to know Barbara, whose professional skill, enthusiasm, and charm were responsible for a delightful television program.

I am pleased that she has carried the project forward into a book, bringing to it all the talent she richly displayed in the earlier phase of this venture.

Louisiana's legacy from those who have gone before us is much greater than ghost tales. Louisiana is blessed with a culture and history that distinguish her from any other state. Her distinction is based on many elements, most of which stem from the various cultures that have so greatly influenced her character.

To those who may be encountering Louisiana for the first time through these wonderful stories—prepare to be engaged and entertained to a degree to which you are certainly unaccustomed. Part of your pleasure will come from the stories themselves and part from the style in which they are presented. Barbara's gift for storytelling holds in the written word just as it does before a television camera.

There is something in the dark, delta soil of Louisiana that leads some visitors to feel a compulsive tug at the sleeves—a signal to return. Small wonder, then, that there would be spirits unable to rest. They, like many of us, just can't imagine leaving Louisiana.

—PHILLIP J. JONES
Secretary, The Louisiana Department
of Culture, Recreation, and Tourism

Preface

In nature nothing dies.
From each sad remnant of decay,
Some forms of life arise.
—Charles Mackay

Ghost, spirit, bogeyman, loup garou, feu follet, pirate, voodoo queen—they come in many guises. Spirits by their very nature do not lend themselves easily to a factual accounting, yet in sultry Louisiana, apparitions are the norm. With a reputation for possessing more ghostly inhabitants than real ones, the Bayou State boasts ghost tales that are legendary and prolific. Ghosts here do not require any manufacturing. *They just are.* Why? *They always have been.* For most residents of Louisiana, this is about all the logical explanation necessary for validation.

The spirits who roam these pages are quirky characters, displaying amazing abilities: the apparition at Loyd Hall in Cheneyville plays the violin; Madewood's poltergeist favors feats of prestidigitation; the Capitol Ghost in Baton Rouge triggers security alarms; the ghostly decorator at the Lanaux Mansion in the French Quarter offers impeccable advice; and like Alice in Wonderland, a little girl is trapped in the mirror at Lafitte Guest House on Bourbon Street.

11

The television documentary *The Haunting of Louisiana* was intended as a showcase for a few of these restless souls. With layer upon layer of ghostly phenomena wandering about, some spirits did not get to prance before the camera—after all a one-hour television program has its limitations. A book format provides more spacious accommodations for these spectral creatures to strut their stuff. Once free, they populated my world. A caveat for the reader: they are poised to take over yours; a belief in the supernatural is not a prerequisite.

The stories gathered here are sprinkled with a few personal notes and observations. Enjoy.

Acknowledgments

All creative endeavors are a collaboration. I am gratefully indebted to those who shared their stories with me: Teeta Moss and Hester Eby at The Myrtles; Naomi Marshall and Keith Marshall at Madewood Plantation; Edith Layton at Ormond Plantation; Marion Hebert at Destrehan Manor; Louis Cornay at Chretien Point; Anne Fitzgerald and Beulah Davis at Loyd Hall; Foster Creppel at Woodland Plantation; Phillip J. Jones, Mary Louise Prudhomme, John Hoover, Wanda Lee Porter, and David Bonaventure at the Old State Capitol; Capt. Jerome Dupré of Chacahoula Tours; Tom Duran of The New Orleans Ghost Tours; Marion Chambon and Alma Neal at The Beauregard-Keyes House; Ruth Bodenheimer at the Lanaux Mansion; Danny O'Flaherty at O'Flaherty's Irish Channel Pub; Ron Waldridge and Frank Loftus at Arnaud's Restaurant; and Irv Zoller at Metairie Cemetery.

A few of the lively spirits in this book first appeared in a short television feature I produced in 1988 for Peggy Scott Laborde's weekly New Orleans show, "Steppin' Out"—many thanks, Peggy. A decade later in 1999, I expanded the idea into a full-length documentary, *The Haunting of Louisiana*, that aired on PBS stations around the country. The accolades all go to my partner in Keepsake Productions, award-winning photographer Oak Lea. It was Oak who first encouraged me to write this book. Thanks also to Joslyn Yeager, former program director of WLAE-TV in New Orleans, now with WLPB in Baton Rouge, for her wise counsel and encouragement. And to Bill Yeager, I truly appreciate your thoughtful reading and comments.

To Danielle, Rebecca, and Heather Genter, who always offer their unconditional support for whatever project their mother goes flitting after—I am indeed fortunate to have such talented and tolerant daughters. A special thanks Danielle for your expert research, tracking down resources and translations in far-flung locales, and for your inspiring photographs.

But above all, Rebecca, my own personal in-house editor, this time I owe it all to you. Your patience and persistence, reading and rereading every word, held me to a higher standard. I would still be wandering aimlessly among my contentious spirits without your talent and skill. I live for your checkmarks of approval!

Any liberties taken with noted figures of the past are all mine. If I have erred, I am confident their spirits will find a way to come back and haunt me.

The
HAUNTING
of
LOUISIANA

1

America's Most Haunted Home

Fingerprints in mirrors, footprints on stairs, pungent aromas, rumpled beds, stolen hair ribbons, death by poison, hanging, and gunfire—The Myrtles Plantation in the West Feliciana town of St. Francisville holds the dubious record of more ghostly phenomena per square inch than anywhere else in the country. Local legend holds that the plantation, built on an ancient Tunica Indian burial mound, was cursed the moment the white man took over.

Crossing through the double French doors of the main house onto the rear verandah, the current owner of The Myrtles, Teeta Moss, pauses briefly to listen to the serenade of a trickling fountain in the courtyard. It is a moment of rare solitude for the proprietress of this popular tourist attraction. The Myrtles plays host to an endless stream of visitors, many lured by stories of restless spirits. Teeta Moss works hard to maintain a balance between The Myrtles' status as a historic home and its more widely held reputation as a haunted house.

Ever vigilant, the retired schoolteacher has not lost the practiced survey of her surroundings. Keen eyes panning from left to right, she sweeps the grounds noting everything is in its appointed place. Before beginning an interview for *The*

Haunting of Louisiana documentary, Mrs. Moss concedes that the soothing ambiance is often at odds with The Myrtles' troubled past. Settling into a white wrought-iron chair on the brick-covered patio, she begins with a factual accounting of the events: "The original 650 acres were part of a 1796 land grant to Revolutionary War general David Bradford. On his death, General Bradford left the estate to his daughter Sara Matilda. Fourteen-year-old Sara married Judge Clarke Woodruff, giving birth to three beautiful daughters."

Teeta's recital paints a vivid portrait of antebellum life in the South. The Woodruff family emerges colorfully dressed in elegant finery. The 500 slaves who labor in the adjoining cotton and indigo fields do not fare as well. Even the additional 40 slaves working indoors as house servants remain anonymous figures—all except for Chloe; for without this young female slave, gifted with a quick mind and a burning ambition, the legend of The Myrtles' ghosts might easily be dismissed.

Taking a slave for a mistress was a common practice among wealthy plantation owners during the pre-Civil War era, and the attractive Chloe was known to be Judge Woodruff's favored concubine. Seeking to increase her influence and power, the clever Chloe gathered information whenever she could. A usually reliable trick was to crack the parlor door open a few inches and eavesdrop on the Judge's private conversations with fellow planters. One awful afternoon, as Judge Woodruff was engaged in a heated argument, Chloe, in her eagerness to hear all the details, pushed the door open a little too far. She was caught. The punishment was cruel and severe. Judge Woodruff ordered her left ear to be cut off, then banished Chloe from the house and back to the fields. Undeterred, Chloe had a plan.

Shaking her no-nonsense wedge of blond hair in disbelief at Chloe's persistence, Teeta describes what happened next. In the gleaming dining room of the main house, preparations were at a peak to celebrate the ninth birthday of the Woodruffs' eldest daughter. With her bloodied head wrapped in a turban,

Chloe snuck into the kitchen. Secretly she concocted a special cake. In the batter she mixed the juices from the oleander leaf, which, explains Teeta, "lets off a liquid similar to arsenic." Chloe knew small doses of this poison would make everyone ill. Her plan was to step in and magically administer a cure. Chloe believed that the grateful Woodruffs would then see her as a powerful voodoo priestess, and she would be allowed to resume her former standing in the home. The scheme had a fatal flaw; in her zeal, Chloe used too much oleander juice. Sara, the Judge's wife, and two of their three innocent children died from eating the poisonous birthday cake.

Like the author of a grim morality play, Teeta Moss unveils the climactic ending: "Chloe in a panic told the other slaves what she had done because she really did not intend to kill Sara and the girls. Out of respect and fear of the Judge, Chloe's fellow servants dragged Chloe outside, and hung her from a large oak tree on the property."

Despite her gruesome punishment, the stubborn spirit of Chloe refuses to leave. Over the years, many visitors claim to have "felt" the presence of Chloe, or blame the ghost of Chloe when objects are missing or misplaced. Hester Eby, a tour guide at The Myrtles through three successive owners, agrees. She is sure the culprit who plucks hair ornaments off the heads of unsuspecting young schoolgirls touring the home is the pesky Chloe. "When they start the tour they have their little clips and ribbons holding their hair, but when they finish the tour, they're gone. We go back and search the rooms, and we can't find them anywhere."

There is a theory circulating at The Myrtles that the conniving Chloe may be trying to get back at the Judge's little daughters for causing her so much grief by eating too much of the poisoned cake; Chloe only picks on the girls on tour—never the boys.

The most substantial proof of Chloe's abiding presence was captured by accident. In December of 1992, John Moss purchased The Myrtles and presented it to his wife, Teeta, as a surprise Christmas gift. The Mosses had been searching for a home in the gentle rolling hills of the Feliciana parishes east of the Mississippi. Their first impression of The Myrtles was a good one. The Myrtles, then operating as a successful bed and breakfast establishment, bore the seal of approval of The National Register of Historic Places. Both John and Teeta looked on The Myrtles' reputation as "America's Most Haunted Home" as merely a great marketing ploy. Neither Teeta nor John were into the occult.

Determined to protect the national ranking of their historic property, they set new guest rules: *No seances. No ouija boards. No ghost busters.* If an overnight guest chose to imagine he saw a spirit flickering by, that was fine; it made for amusing conversation over morning coffee and croissants. However, active pursuit by paranormal practitioners was strictly prohibited.

Shortly after moving in, Teeta took pictures to document the proximity of adjacent buildings to the home for a fire-code rating. She sent off a few copies to the insurance company, absentmindedly leaving the remaining packet of photographs on a table in the adjoining restaurant. An alert employee noticed something curious in one of the photos. A slim turbaned female form could be seen lurking in the passageway between the main house and the old kitchen building. The staff member was unnerved—the figure in the photo was transparent; the clapboard siding of the house was clearly visible *through* her body. Teeta Moss was dubious. Convinced it must be a defect or shadow, she carefully checked the remaining photos. Taken from widely different angles, they all revealed the same shadowy image. There were so many requests to see "the lurking ghost" that the photo was eventually turned into an advertising postcard for The Myrtles.

The postcard itself attracted the attention of a visitor who felt it warranted a closer examination. He blew it up and took some measurements. He found the dimensions of "The Shadow" to conform exactly to a human body—specifically female—from the width of the shoulders, to the length of the neck, to the circumference of the head. The detailed scrutiny of the photo held a few more surprises—two to be exact—silhouettes of two small children kneeling on the roof of the main house!

Teeta Moss has no rational explanation. "That can really just raise the hair on the back of your neck when you look at that because it is so real." In a clear and precise voice, Teeta swears that, when she took the pictures, it was a quiet Sunday morning. *No one* was on the grounds. There were *no signs* of any woman anywhere about, and Teeta is absolutely certain that there were *no children* perched on the roof. An enlargement of the original photo, with measurements marked in red, is on display at The Myrtles for those who wish to draw their own conclusions.

The ghosts of this centuries-old raised Creole cottage are not camera shy. Indeed, they seem to favor the spotlight. Tour guide Hester Eby refers to another bizarre photo as "The Coffin Picture." Hester, clad in a brightly flowered muumuu and rocking to and fro in a wicker rocker on the back gallery, peppers her conversation with broad smiles and low laughs. Her charming demeanor belies the chilling details of The Myrtles' tragic history. Hester explains that the picture she is holding was taken by one of the overnight guests as she took an evening stroll near the pond behind the home.

The picture is in color, but the figures are hazy. Hester's vivid description rapidly brings ethereal shapes into focus: "There are about six or so men dressed in colonial clothing. They look as if they are carrying something like a coffin, and the men are positioned like pallbearers at a funeral." Hester points to a row of white rectangular-shaped objects in the upper left-hand section of the picture: "Over here by the pond there's nothing but headstones. It looks like a burial ground." Hester pauses, allowing for that precise measure of time it takes for an icy sliver of fear to travel across the shoulder blades and down the spine. "Here there are legs. When you follow the legs up, the rest of the body is connected to a branch."

Like the winning prosecutor in a murder trial, Hester triumphantly flashes the photo, "People's Exhibit A," a double image of death: the infamous Chloe at her hanging, and the funeral of the original owner, Revolutionary War general David Bradford.

If the jury has any lingering doubts as to the existence of ghosts in this mansion, Hester presents further tangible evidence. Rising from her wicker throne on the gallery, she unlocks the doors to the main house, on the way to "People's Exhibits B and C." Hester positions herself next to a large, ornate, gilded mirror dominating the front hall. "They were so superstitious in the early 1800s—not only here at The Myrtles, but throughout the South—they strongly believed that whenever someone died on the plantation grounds, that all mirrors needed to be covered with a black cloth. If they weren't covered, the spirit of the deceased could enter the mirror and be trapped in the home." Hester's storytelling effortlessly transports her audience back to an earlier era. "During the time of the poisoning of Sara and her daughters, there was so much confusion that this mirror was left uncovered. It's believed those people's souls still live inside this section of the mirror."

For added emphasis, Hester lays her hand on the mirror, index finger pointing to dark discolorations in the glass bearing a marked resemblance to small handprints. The Clarence Darrow of tour guides slowly traces the mirror's evolution step by step. "This is the original frame; the glass looks very old, but it's not. It was replaced eight years ago, and each time a new glass has been placed back into that frame, the handprints reappear."

Hester's presentation is far from done. It's time for "People's Exhibit C." Hester flips over an 8x10 on the hall table under the mirror. "A lot of people say you can pick up faces in this mirror. This picture was taken by one of our guests, and there's a lady on the staircase." Hester indicates a spot midway in the photo. "You can see her body clearly reflected in the mirror. The guest is positive there was no one on the staircase when she took the picture." Hester's large brown eyes dare you to doubt in the face of these facts.

For one couple from New Orleans, an unsettling experience with a troublesome ghost happened in a bedroom just a few feet across the hall from the mysterious "Mirror, Mirror, on the Wall." Totally unaware of the plantation's haunted reputation, Dr. Peter Tufton booked a room for himself and his wife, Linda. Arriving late for their quiet weekend getaway, the Tuftons went immediately to their room adjacent to the front hall.

The dentist's sleep was interrupted in the early morning hours by a discordant melody running through his head. Slowly he sat up, trying not to disturb his wife, but a few seconds later she too sat up, asking what was going on. Her husband replied he thought he heard music. Linda Tufton turned to her husband and hummed a tune. "Does it go like this?" she asked. The Tuftons were amazed to discover that although they both had heard the same melody in their sleep, it was not audible in the room.

The Tuftons' nocturnal discussion about their puzzling wakeup call was interrupted by the sound of footsteps crashing down the red-carpeted staircase outside their door. Getting up to check, they saw another tormented couple, suitcases in hand, storming out of the house, shouting that the "ghosts" wouldn't leave them alone.

The next morning the Tuftons learned they were sleeping in the room of "The Rumpled Bed." A bemused Teeta Moss confirms that no matter how many times housekeeping straightens the linens, "someone" returns to rumple the covers. "It looks like somebody's been in the bed," says Teeta, demonstrating by lying on the bedspread, then getting up and leaving the impression of her body in the covers. "This is the morning room, where the mistress of the plantation took care of the servants, like being the mayor of a small village. . . . She worked hard to run a large plantation." Speculation abounds that this room is a battleground between the spirit of Chloe, who leaves her imprint on the bed in defiance of her former mistress, and the fastidious

Sara Woodruff, who struggles to maintain order. If there is a third spirit claiming squatter's rights to the room by humming a haunted tune, his identity is oddly unknown; the origin of most ghostly phenomena at The Myrtles is easier to trace.

Ghostly footsteps in the night, for example, are attributed to William Winter, son-in-law of the Sterlings, the third owners. Contrary to the disquieting experience of the sleep-deprived Tuftons, the echo of pounding feet is usually heard going up the stairs, not down.

One calm winter morning as William was playing with his young son in the front parlor, a man on horseback rode up calling for the lawyer, William Winter. William strode out onto the gallery, leaning over the intricate design of the cast-iron railing to meet the visitor. William was greeted with a shotgun blast to his chest. Staggering inside, he attempted to reach his beloved wife on the second floor. The fatally wounded William only made it to the seventeenth step, where he collapsed and died. Numerous guests at The Myrtles speak of hearing a lady's voice cry out for William, and footsteps stumbling up the staircase but never coming back down.

Teeta Moss elects to change the direction of such stories, preferring to talk of less violent reminders of The Myrtles' past. "There was a Confederate soldier who lived here for awhile, and we often smell cigar smoke in the house, real pungent cigar smoke—and there's no smoking allowed at The Myrtles."

Another inexplicable incident she fondly recalls occurred when a friend and her two small children arrived for a visit with the Mosses' two young sons. They all decided to share the same upstairs bedroom. "Around 10:30 that night, the room filled with a sweet, sweet, perfume smell, like jungle gardenia, that sweet. Of course I thought it was my friend playing a joke, and I accused her of spraying perfume. She said, 'No, I promise I didn't. I thought it was you.' Then the room just became frigid, like a freezer, that cold. This was in August of 1994." Underscoring the obvious, Teeta adds with eyebrows raised, "Nothing is frigid in August in Louisiana."

Teeta Moss also mentions times when "you'll hear your name called by a familiar voice. I'll think my husband is calling me, and I'll start looking for him. I'll ask the staff where he is, and they'll say, 'Why, Miss Teeta, Johnny went to the bank. He's not here.'" Teeta's tales are punctuated with rolls of her denim-blue eyes and how-can-you-explain-that shrugs.

And what about *tour guide extraordinaire* Hester Eby? Has she ever had any personal encounters of the ghostly variety? Hester confesses that when she first applied for a job at *The Haunted House* she was leery, but she needed the work. Initially she found there was one spot—behind the velvet-covered settee in the gentleman's parlor—that made her especially uncomfortable.

Tour guides are given specific instructions to stand behind the sofa when leading groups through this room, so as not to block the view of the furnishings. Unfortunately for Hester, this small space between the window and the settee is also a favored cubbyhole for a diminutive spirit. "I've been pulled on slightly on my dress or my skirt, as if a child is trying to get my attention." Hester reports that the "ghost child" persists in tugging at her whenever she tries to stand in the designated docent spot.

Throughout her years of service at The Myrtles, Hester's direct dealings with ghosts had been limited to minor spectral displays—doors locking and unlocking, missing hair ribbons, disembodied voices, ghostly giggles—nothing overtly evil or threatening. But in the spring of 1998, Hester had her first real face-to-face encounter with a ghost.

It was eight A.M. The Moss family was sleeping upstairs in their private quarters. Hester was the first staff member to arrive and so began the daily routine of opening the gift shop on the first floor. As she lifted the latch on the screen door to put food on the porch for Myrt, the current resident black cat, Hester spotted a car looping its way up the circular drive. The visitors parked and got out. Hester saw a man, woman, and little girl. Hester went back inside as the family approached the gift-shop entrance. The couple came in and the woman asked for tickets for two adults. Hester inquired about a ticket for their daughter. The woman replied that there was only her husband and herself. Thinking perhaps the child had remained on the porch to look at a nanny doll resting on a stool outside the door, Hester sold the couple their tickets, then went out to check on the child. The cuddly nanny doll stared blankly back at Hester. No little girl had picked her up for a hug. A thorough search of the porch, parking lot, and couple's car revealed no signs of the child.

Hester is adamant she saw a little girl skipping behind the couple. "She had long blond hair and a black and white dress complete with pantaloons. She was about eight or nine years old." Nodding her head in quiet acceptance, Hester slides the pieces of the puzzle together: "She was the same age as the oldest daughter of the Woodruffs when she died from eating too much poison in her birthday cake."

Years of dealing with the antics of the spirits at The Myrtles have conditioned Hester Eby to take a good-natured approach. "There's nothing you can do." With a generous smile Hester adds, "It's their home as well. They're not afraid of you, and you shouldn't be afraid of them because they're not here to harm anyone. It's just where they live. The Myrtles is over two hundred years old. Things do happen."

2

Ghostly Lagniappe

In French Louisiana, the word "lagniappe" refers to a small gift, a little extra bonus. Little did Teeta Moss suspect that when her husband, John, gave her The Myrtles Plantation it came packaged with an additional measure of protection. A friend of Teeta's, the owner of an adjacent historic property, forewarned the new homeowners that any ghosts in residence "will let you know if you are welcome or not."

As the mother of two young sons, a two-year-old and a ten-month-old, Teeta was concerned more about real-world physical dangers than tales of ghoulies and ghosties. "I started to get panicked about the fact that there's this huge open pond behind the house; there are a number of large tour buses arriving daily where the drivers get out and often leave the diesel engines running; there are cars coming in and out all day—there were so many ways a child could get hurt."

Teeta's face furrows as she thinks back to one harrowing morning shortly after moving in. "I was in my office. My ten-month-old, Morgan, was napping, and the nanny was doing the laundry. The nanny had on a baby monitor so she could hear Morgan. All of a sudden, I had this urge that I just couldn't make go away. I kept feeling like I needed to check on the baby.

Finally I turned off the computer, got up, walked out, and just when I looked across the courtyard, there was Morgan about thirty feet from the pond."

Teeta reiterates: "Now, he's ten and a half months old. He's been walking for only three weeks, and somehow he has gotten off a big antique bed, walked across two rooms with enormous heavy doors, crossed the verandah, and traipsed another 100 feet to the pond." Teeta says they checked later and there was nothing wrong with the nanny's baby monitor. No one heard him. No one saw him move. "When I looked over and saw Morgan heading towards the edge of the pond, I just froze and screamed for Nona, his nanny." According to Teeta, in that terrifying instant as she envisioned her young son drowning before her eyes, incredibly her fears vanished. "It was like a cape of warm velvet or velour. It was just real soft and fuzzy, like I was wrapped in it, and there was an enormous sense of comfort. Nothing actually touched me. It was all sensation, but it was so real. I could almost hear a voice saying, *You'll never have to worry—your children, your family—you will always be safe here.*"

This cautious mother affirms that while the incident was painful, she was never again afraid for the children to play on the grounds. Teeta quickly adds, "We do have a fence around the pond now. The good Lord only helps if you help yourself."

Teeta Moss's baptism into the realm of the surreal was reaffirmed shortly after settling in. "One morning I was changing Morgan's diaper in the nanny's room, and my two-year-old was in my bedroom. J.G. (John Gabriel) had climbed on my bed and started crying for me to come and get the little girl off the chandelier." The exchange between mother and son was remarkable:

"Uk, uk, uk—Mommy, she's going to fall!"

"J.G., there's no one there, sweetie."

"Mommy, she's going to fall."

"J.G., what do you see?"

"Uk, Mommy, the pretty girl."

"What color is her hair?"

"Wellow."

"What does she have on?"

"A wedding dress."

Translating for her child, Mrs. Moss states that to J.G. any lacy dress is a wedding dress. Trying to remain calm, this concerned parent gently asked her agitated son, what would he like Mommy to do? Would he like Mommy to ask her to get down? J.G.'s simple answer was "Please, Mommy."

Mrs. Moss complied. "So I'm asking the little girl, whom I can't see, to get down and our nanny walks in and says, 'Miss Teeta, are you okay?'" Teeta smiles in dazed wonder as she relives the memory. "I thought—we've been here three weeks, and the entire staff will think I'm crazy."

For Teeta this was only the incredible beginning of the ongoing relationships between her child and ghostly manifestations. Two weeks after J.G. called for his mother to get the little girl off the chandelier, he revealed his acquaintance with yet another spirit.

The entire Moss family was in the restaurant across the courtyard from the main house when J.G. looked out and announced, "Oh, Mommy, there's my friend!"

Mrs. Moss turned to her son and asked him, "Who, baby?"

"Him, him."

Says Teeta, it was obvious her two-year-old again thought she could see the same person he was seeing. Bending over her son, she cautiously prodded, "Well, I don't see who you are talking about, sweetie. You're going to have to show Mommy where he is."

"Mommy, he's right there. He's dressed like Poppy."

Teeta Moss follows her little son's logic. "My father, who J.G. calls 'Poppy,' always wears overalls." The innocent association of a simple pair of overalls, shared by both grandfather and ghost, offered a tantalizing clue to the identity of J.G.'s ghostly pal.

Drawing on years of research and the preparation of daily lesson plans, Teeta took on the daunting task of documenting The Myrtles' early history. She learned that after the murder of his wife and two of his daughters by the scheming slave Chloe, Judge Clarke Woodruff could not bear to remain at the plantation. The Judge took his only surviving daughter, Octavia, to New Orleans and left the estate in the hands of a trusted caretaker. Eight years later, the caretaker was murdered in a suspected robbery attempt. To her astonishment, Teeta discovered that the caretaker was fond of wearing a faded pair of overalls. J.G.'s "new friend" appeared to be the elderly caretaker who looked after the home some two hundred years ago!

When J.G. pointed out his ghostly buddy to his mother, Mrs. Moss tried to make light of it, and jokingly asked her son if his friend would like to eat with them. J.G. promptly jumped up out of his chair and crossed into the courtyard. "We could see him looking up talking to someone we couldn't see." When J.G. came back and sat down with his family his mother again asked him, "Where is your friend?"

J.G. replied, "He not hungry."

Mrs. Moss says, for her child, it was that simple. The current maintenance man at The Myrtles confirms, "He [J.G.] sees the old caretaker all the time; he's forever talking to him and he's forever telling me to look at him too." What the staff also noted was that as he walked and happily chatted with "his friend," J.G. always cocked his head upwards and lifted his hand in the air as if he was holding on to a tall adult figure.

Unlike Teeta's sons, Hester Eby's daughter, Bell, is no longer comfortable visiting her mother at work. When Hester first started her job at The Myrtles, six-year-old Bell Eby begged to come too. Reluctantly Hester agreed; she picked a slow day after the winter holidays when no visitors were scheduled to arrive. Soon bored within the confines of a house overflowing with antiques, the fun-loving Bell wandered outside in search of something more lively to occupy her time.

Down by the pond, Bell was delighted to come upon another lonely little girl her age. Their giggles transformed the dreary day as they played hide and seek, darting from tree to tree. Abruptly the game ended; Bell trudged up to the house to find her mother. Bell told Hester that her new playmate wanted to borrow her coat and asked if it was okay to share. A surprised Hester firmly told Bell that the house and grounds were empty; mother and daughter were the only two people at The Myrtles. Bell insisted she had been playing with another little girl who was very cold—"She's turning blue, Mommy"— and needed a coat. Unable to convince Bell that she did not need to take her coat off on such a chilly day and give it away, a worried Hester called Bell's father to come and take her home. Hester Eby remains convinced her daughter's playmate was not of this world. "Children do see things, more than adults, you know."

Prompted by these incidents, Teeta Moss decided to tackle some further homework and find out everything she could about spirits who seek out children, and children who interact with spirits. She sought the advice of Elisabeth Kübler-Ross, renowned for her work with terminally ill patients and author of the insightful book, *On Death and Dying*. What Teeta uncovered in her investigation is that a two-year-old can fib, but he cannot conjure. He can take a cookie out of a cookie jar and, while he's munching on the cookie, deny he took it. But normal two-year-olds cannot create—make up something that is not there, something of which they have no previous knowledge. Normal two-year-olds are developmentally incapable of making up stories with such vivid detail. Mrs. Moss says her son J.G. is just an average everyday American boy, not blessed with any special extrasensory gifts.

This perplexed mother can only conclude that spirits from the past—a little girl on the chandelier, an elderly gentleman in the courtyard, a playmate in need of a coat—for reasons far beyond the everyday order of things, did indeed make themselves known to the children. Teeta also chooses to look on spirits who have an affinity for children as guardian angels— ghostly lagniappe of the best kind.

3

Solitary Apparitions

Far from the madding crowd of spirits at The Myrtles, two other historic homes each lay claim to only a single manifestation. Oak Alley's "Lady of Illusion" and "The Poltergeist" at Madewood Plantation prefer to haunt in solitary splendor.

The palatial grandeur of Oak Alley Plantation reigns over the west bank of the Mississippi River in Vacherie. Lining the entrance is a commanding avenue of twenty-eight sheltering live oak trees, hailed as the most photographed avenue of trees in the world. A couple from Texas who set out to take a few souvenir photos of their own captured more than most. Their photo of the master bedroom created quite a stir.

Oak Alley's master bedroom has been restored to the period of the original owners. It was the domain of Jacques Telesphore Roman and his Creole bride, the lovely Celina. Peering over the Plexiglas barriers, tourists are able to catch a glimpse of a typical day in 1837: Sunbeams stream through the windows, showering the room with sparkling highlights. A mahogany breakfast tray rests on the carved pineapple tester bed; the lace-edged covers are turned down. The master and mistress have just finished their early-morning ritual of café au lait and sugary beignets while the newest addition to the

Roman family sleeps peacefully in his elaborate rosewood cradle. In the far corner, a mannequin is draped in the mistress's latest outfit, awaiting madam's pleasure.

Mesmerized by the scene before them, Mr. and Mrs. Larry Bernard of Fort Worth, Texas quickly snap several pictures, hoping to capture the magical scene. They are wildly successful. One photo reveals the figure of a slight young woman serenely standing and staring out of the French doors to the avenue of oaks below. Masses of thick dark hair cascade down her back.

Closer examination of the snapshot does little to explain her odd presence. She is visible in the photo, but her reflection in the mirror is minus a head. The Bernards lingered at the end of the tour; they saw no one else in the master bedroom suite when they took their pictures. The couple sent the mystifying photo back to Oak Alley, hoping the staff could offer some explanation of how a nonexistent woman posed for their camera and lost her head.

The staff could only shrug and suggest that perhaps "the lady" was merely a distortion of the headless dressmaker's form. If so, where did the head adorned with dark curls come from, and how did it pop up in the photo? French revolutionaries were famous for crying, "Off with her head!"—however, this was a case study in reverse dynamics. A headless mannequin was caught with her head intact.

In Louisiana, the land of dreamy dreams, this now-you-see-her, now-you-don't "Lady of Illusion" may very well be the lovely Celina Roman, slipping back into the home she fondly called *Bon Séjour*—Pleasant Sojourn. For Celina was as entranced with the "Legacy of the Avenue of Oaks" as others had been before her.

The legacy began with the legend of a mysterious French settler. In the early 1700s, lured by the promise of colonial opulence, he built a crude cabin on this site. Dreaming one day of a palatial home, he planted twenty-eight tiny oak saplings to create a magnificent entrance. The harsh economics of rural life shattered his dream; his grand palace was not to be, and the unknown visionary faded from the scene.

By the 1830s the picture changed dramatically. Sugarcane ushered in a flood of ready cash. François Gabriel ("Valcour") Aimé, "The Sugar King of Louisiana," purchased this tract of land, which river travelers and steamboat captains dubbed "Oak Alley" after the now-imposing quarter-mile avenue of towering oaks. In 1836 Valcour, brother-in-law and friend of Celina's husband, Jacques, made the newlyweds an offer they couldn't refuse.

Enthusiastically the couple purchased the coveted land and plunged into building their dream home. Only the best would do. Celina's father, the architect Gilbert Joseph Pilié, designed a home for his daughter that would mirror the grandeur of the legendary oaks. Pilié surrounded the house with twenty-eight classic Doric columns—one column for each of the twenty-eight trees—a tribute to the nameless creator of "Oak Alley." Sadly, like the unknown French settler before her, Celina's stay in this place of tranquil beauty was short-lived.

Tragedy struck in 1848. Celina's beloved husband, Jacques, died, a victim of tuberculosis. The widow Celina was devastated. Unable to cope with the management of a large country estate, she was forced to sell. The plantation went on the auction block, lost forever to the Roman family.

There is conjecture that, like the slave Chloe at The Myrtles, Celina can never fully abandon her former home. If Celina Roman is indeed the "Lady of Illusion" slipping in on occasion to primp before the mirror, who can blame her?

At the opposite end of the ghostly spectrum, the quiet demeanor of Oak Alley's tragic mistress is overpowered by the flamboyant display at another nearby plantation. This lively spirit indulges in startling feats of prestidigitation. His favorite haunt is the dining room of Madewood, a Greek Revival manor gracing the banks of Bayou Lafourche in Napoleonville.

Sugar and cotton plantations were huge operations. Each was a complex unto itself, with the requisite manor house, overseer's

house, slave quarters, barns, sugar mills, pigeon cotes, plantation store, hospital dispensary, blacksmith shop, and small
chapel—often resembling miniature kingdoms. Governing over
all with unquestioned authority was the sugar baron himself,
with as many as a thousand slaves providing the backbone for
this feudal economy. Over time most of the ancillary buildings
fell into decay and were lost, but a few of the grandiose manor
homes have survived due to extensive preservation efforts.

New Orleans gallery owner and art consultant Naomi
Marshall purchased Madewood in 1964 and immediately set
about restoring the main house to its former glory. The original construction of the 1840s mansion spanned four years, uti-
lizing 60,000 slave-made bricks. The temple-like facade
features six fluted Ionic columns and diamond-shaped balus-
ters wrapping the upper gallery.

Resplendent in a deep-purple suit, gleaming white hair precisely coifed, eighty-year-old Naomi Marshall regally holds
court in the parlor, recalling the monumental task of removing
decades of debris from the home's interior. The pigeon drop-
pings and accumulated mold were so encrusted on the walls
and ceilings, Naomi determined the only practical method to
clean house was to take a hose to it.

One day early in the cleaning process stands out from the
rest. Naomi remembers wearing a bathing suit, head wrapped
in a kerchief, spraying water up the carved interior stairwell,
when a man drove up and said, "I'd love to see the house."
Graciously Naomi obliged. She put down her hose and invited
him inside. As they stood under the peeling ceiling and crumbling walls, their conversation revealed how perilously close
Madewood had come to meeting a permanent demise.

The stranger announced: "I'm surely sorry you got this
house before I could."

Curious Naomi inquired, "What would you have done with it?"

Shaking his head in profound regret over his loss, the
stranger responded: "The money I could have gotten for the
brick and timber."

Naomi Marshall wasted no time ushering the demolition expert to the door, informing him that his "tour was over." To some, progress is moving forward.

To most in Louisiana, progress is ensuring that the past is alive and well, and that there is always a place at the table for family—even the dearly departed.

When Naomi Marshall signed the papers for Madewood, she bought it lock, stock—and cemetery. Although she was pleased to find that it came replete with the original Pugh family tombs, she had not counted on one of the deceased joining them for dinner.

Guarded by an ancient army of stalwart oaks, the Pugh family cemetery lies tucked about three hundred yards behind the main house. Dripping from gnarled limbs, tendrils of graying Spanish moss caress the tips of the tallest tombs. A gentle breeze wafts to and fro. Defying gravity, a rust-speckled iron fence leans precariously inward, as if unseen hands are gathering it close to protect their last vestige of privacy. Since 1846 Col. Thomas Pugh, his wife, Eliza Foley, their children, and their children's children have slept here side by side, their whispered secrets caught in the languid air.

While Naomi and her family wisely left the tombs themselves untouched, they did clear away mounds of tangled weeds and rotting wood. One disgruntled soul, possibly Colonel Pugh himself, was clearly not pleased with the new unobstructed view, and the ensuing visitors. A little retaliation, it seems, was in order. To make his objections known, the ghost decided to see how the Marshalls would react to a little rearrangement at one of *their* family gatherings.

Naomi Marshall describes the evening when the grumpy ghost commanded their attention with some unusual table manners. "We were all sitting around talking and laughing after a big dinner. I had a magnificent cranberry epergne [glass centerpiece] on the buffet. All of a sudden the epergne just lifted up and came down on the floor." Mrs. Marshall raises her arms to demonstrate the levitation of the priceless family heirloom.

Fortunately for the Marshalls the ghost was not too vindictive, carefully avoiding any permanent damage. "It was amazing," Mrs. Marshall declared. "Not a chip was broken off of it." Despite the dramatic display of disapproval by the pesky poltergeist, the Marshalls remain convinced that their restoration efforts have ensured Madewood's very survival for future generations to enjoy. Colonel Pugh's portrait now hangs prominently in a downstairs hallway; neither the Marshalls nor their bed and breakfast guests have reported any recent signs of furrowed brows, frowns, disapproving sighs, or, alas—to the disappointment of avid ghost lovers—further feats of prestidigitation.

4

What Else Do They Leave Behind?

By their very nature, antebellum homes are repositories of the past. Many a soul has passed through the portals of a 200-year-old plantation. Edith Layton, a former docent at Ormond Plantation, poses a provocative question: "With so many occupants stamping a variety of emotions upon this particular environment, if it's possible to leave fingerprints, what else is left behind?"

What else indeed? Ormond Plantation, in St. Charles Parish on the east bank of the mighty Mississippi near Destrehan, is full of dark secrets. Completed in 1790, the Louisiana colonial-style home was part of a land grant awarded to Pierre Trepagnier by the Spanish governor of the Louisiana territories, Don Bernardo de Galvez. The lavish home was often the setting for elaborate parties in honor of visiting dignitaries. In 1798 sugar baron Pierre Trepagnier vanished without a trace, leaving his children haunted by a father they would never know.

One evening while the Trepagniers were at dinner, a servant entered the room to inform the master that a coach with a Spanish insignia on the door had driven up to the property. Pierre got up to see. When the servant checked, his master and the phantom coach had mysteriously disappeared. No trace of

Pierre Trepagnier was ever found, although one medium feels she may have been in contact.

In the 1990s, the restored Ormond Plantation once again played gracious host and was the scene for a special function for visiting hospitality-industry executives. As part of the evening's entertainment, a voodoo demonstration and seance were in progress. The china and silverware on the dining-room table were removed, and the medium spread her accoutrements across the polished mahogany surface. In the center of the table, she placed a small incense dish to ward off evil spirits. To set the proper period mood for the guests, Edith Layton, Ormond's business manager, donned full antebellum finery—blue taffeta bouffant gown, red hair piled high, cameo necklace on black-velvet ribbon—the quintessential Southern dame. Lighting the candles, Edith began with the tale of Pierre Trepagnier's untimely disappearance. "When I got to the part about Pierre walking out the door and his family never seeing him again, the little incense dish cracked with a loud pop, right on cue." Smiling Edith Layton adds, "I thought it was effective."

Other masters of Ormond Plantation seemed doomed to follow the tragic fate of Pierre. On June 25, 1805, Col. Richard Butler bought the house and land from the widow Trepagnier. He rechristened the home Ormond, taking the name from his ancestral property, the Castle Ormonde in Ireland. Colonel Butler did not have long to savor his latest acquisition. Terrified by the dreaded yellow fever that was ravaging the local populace, he sold Ormond in 1819, fleeing with his wife to what he believed was the healthier climate of Bay St. Louis, Mississippi—but escape was futile. The fever followed and took Richard Butler in his prime, at forty-three.

Ormond drifted through a series of owners after the War Between the States. In 1898, Louisiana state senator Basile LaPlace, Jr., hoped to transform Ormond into a profitable rice-producing operation. Less than a year later, he made an untimely and gruesome exit. On October 11, 1899, the senator's body, hit by a barrage of bullets, was found hanging from a massive oak tree hugging a curve on the Great Mississippi River Road.

Edith Layton says local legends differ regarding the perpetrators of the crime. "Some feel because of his political position, the senator made an enemy in the Ku Klux Klan, and the Klan killed him. Others think he was philandering with the caretaker's daughter, and it was the caretaker and his son that sought revenge." Ms. Layton states that these theories have never been proven. The only facts not in dispute are the unfortunate deaths of three men, their harrowing exits all preceded by their entrance into Ormond's hallowed halls. Ormond's ominous history is layered with tragic tales of hauntings by hapless victims and with baffling paranormal phenomena.

One of Edith Layton's personal favorites has an ironic twist. "I was leading a group of ladies on tour, and one lady in particular kept asking me about ghosts. I decided to humor her and tell her some of things that I had heard. Every time I would pause, she would punctuate the sentence by declaring, 'That's a ghost for you!' as if she was on familiar terms with every ghost who ever wandered by."

Edith's husky voice drops to a conspiratorial tone as she divulges what happened next. "At this point we're standing on the verandah and to my right I hear this deafening noise. I turned my head away while the lady is still talking, which is extremely rude, and look down the porch to see what's making the racket. Pretty soon the noise roars towards us. Something goes *through* me. My knees buckle. My mind is going, *What's that? What's that?"*

Edith says on recovering, she spun back around to check on the ladies. They appeared unscathed by the strange phenomenon. "Here this lady is still blithering on about her knowledge of the spirit world, and she hasn't heard or felt a thing." Edith's booming laugh highlights the absurdity of her predicament.

Edith Layton no longer works as a full-time tour guide; she leaves the ghost hunting to others. "People would ask me, 'Is this house haunted?' and I would normally reply, 'They work a different shift!'" Or so Ms. Layton fervently hopes, for the ghosts at Ormond, as elsewhere in Louisiana, have their own agenda, unencumbered by time and space.

5

A Finger-Pointing Ghost and Buried Treasure

Shimmering slivers of moonbeams pierce the canopy of oaks circling the old manor house. A burst of chill air blows in from the river, lifting the craggy branches and shaking the leaves in an eerie ballet. Two deckhands clamber up the levee, returning to a tug moored on the river embankment. Glancing over his shoulder, the younger of the two speculates on what he'd do if he owned a plantation like the one behind them. "I'd sit out there on that porch, put my feet up, snap my fingers for somebody to fetch me a drink, and count my money!"

"And you'd need a lot of it if you lived there," counters his companion, clutching his windbreaker tighter around his ample chest.

"What is your problem, Joe? Wouldn't you like to be rich for once in your life?"

"Yeah, but I wouldn't want me a big monster house like that one. There wouldn't be enough money in the world to keep fixing the leaks in the roof and replacing the bricks on all those damn chimneys every time a hurricane roared by."

"You know what, Joe? I bet if someone handed you a treasure map right now, you'd complain about how you'd have to go get a shovel, dig a lot of holes, move a bunch of dirt, and when you finally found the treasure, then you'd complain some more, because you'd have to hire somebody to guard it 'cause people would want to steal it." The young

deckhand is feeling pretty cocky after a night on the town and enjoys ribbing his pessimistic friend.

The two drinking buddies have taken a zigzag route to the top of the levee. The lights from the wheelhouse of the tugboat Cruisin' Cajun *illuminate the stretch of riverbank in front of the old plantation. Looking out at the muddy waters as they rest at the top of the levee, Joe nudges Rene. "Hey, dreamer, next you're gonna tell me that patch of fog on the river is some kind of spook or ghost."*

Rene squints in the direction Joe is looking, about fifty yards out. "Well, it does have kind of a weird shape to it."

"Man, you're nuts." Joe plods downhill towards the string of barges guarded by the tug.

"Joe, wait. Wait! The fog thing, one part of it is sticking out . . . like . . . a hand. . . . I'm serious . . . it's like it's pointing to the big house . . . maybe there's some buried treasure there!"

An impatient captain steps out of the wheelhouse, watching his over-due deckhands stagger back. "What are you two yammering about? The wind is picking up and I need you to check the lines."

Hustling on board, Joe nods his head back to Rene. "Oh, Boy Wonder there is seein' things. Ghosts walking on water."

The captain fixes a hard stare at the river, then as if his head is stuck on a rusty turret, he cranks it starboard in jerky increments till his eyes zero in on the old plantation house. "I've had my fill of ghosts and buried treasure," grumbles the captain. Wheeling his considerable frame back to port, he announces, "Nobody ever found anything." Abruptly slamming the door of the wheelhouse behind him, the captain leaves his deckhands puzzled over his curious remarks.

Destrehan Manor, on the east bank of the river above New Orleans, is the oldest documented plantation house in the lower Mississippi Valley. Under the guardianship of the River Road Historical Society, the former private home is open to the public. Costumed docents warmly welcome most visitors, but a ban on ghosts is strictly enforced.

The prohibition on apparitions is purely a practical one. While other historic sites capitalized on the marketing appeal of their alleged haunted status, rumors of a finger-pointing ghost nearly destroyed Destrehan Manor.

Peering from behind a black veil and bonnet, *de rigueur* accessories for her eighteenth-century mourning costume, museum docent Marion Hebert is visibly upset. "Destrehan is the only plantation I know of that has suffered damage, physical damage, from a ghost."

Fueled by a local legend of the phantom pirate Jean Lafitte purportedly pointing to a secret cache of buried treasure, looters went on a rampage, nearly annihilating the historic structure in their quest for gold. Ascending the staircase, the fiercely protective docent denounces the grave impact on Destrehan as "rape." Leading the way to an unrestored second-floor bedroom, Marion demonstrates what the house looked like when the vandals were done. The *bousillage* (mud and moss insulation) was left exposed; holes were dug in the floors and ceilings; marble mantels were ripped out. The entire home was in danger of collapse, all because of an oft-repeated tale of a finger-pointing ghost.

"The story I heard," says Ms. Hebert, her black gown sweeping behind, "is the ghost of the pirate Jean Lafitte is in the house pointing to the fireplace, showing where he buried his treasure." Adjusting the lace-edged veil in front of her face, Marion laughs. "To me that story is absolutely silly. I mean, if you had money, you wouldn't hide it inside a plantation, go off, and then come back later expecting it would still be there. Surely somebody's going to find that. We all remember when the Yankees were coming. People back then ran out and buried their silver, jewels, and money in the yard thinking they [the Yankees] were too stupid to find it. We all know better than that!"

Marion Hebert is clearly not impressed with the flawed tactics of her Southern ancestors. Nor does Marion think it logical that any self-respecting ghost, especially the one of the crafty pirate Jean Lafitte, would randomly appear in front of strangers and let them know today was their lucky day. Gathering her skirts to begin the descent back to the first floor, Ms. Herbert underscores the futility of the vandals' efforts. "They found no treasure because it was never here." Supported by the stalwart eyes of the Destrehan family patriarch glowering down from his portrait, Marion Hebert is unwavering in her stance. "A man like Jean Noel Destrehan would never have welcomed a man of Jean Lafitte's character into his home."

In 1971 the River Road Historical Society came to the rescue of the abandoned plantation, promptly declaring it a "Ghost-Free Zone." Intent on preserving her historic integrity, society members swore misguided treasure hunters would never again tear her apart.

That's it then, end of story? No pirate (dead or alive) on the premises? No buried treasure?

Unfortunately for the preservationists, vehement denials did little to alleviate the rumors. The specter of the pirate Jean Lafitte hovering over Destrehan led many in the community, like the tugboat captain and his deckhand, to believe that a chest filled with sparkling gems and gold doubloons was within their grasp, if only they were the first to find it.

Jean Lafitte biographer Lyle Saxon cautions that the centuries-old quest for Lafitte's lost treasure encompasses the entire thousand-mile stretch of the Gulf of Mexico, covering "every bay, inlet and bayou from Key West to the mouth of the Rio Grande." Chances of pinpointing the exact location are slim, but for diehards, as long as there is ghost lore to follow, there is hope.

Unquestionably, having endured a series of dramatic reincarnations, Destrehan Manor, the Grand Dame of the Great Mississippi River Road in St. Charles Parish, possesses a certain mystique. From 1802 to 1910, she was home to generations of the wealthy Destrehan family. Like other Southern plantations during the Civil War, she was seized and occupied by Union forces. After the war she underwent a short tenure as a training school for ex-slaves run by the Freedman's Bureau called the Rost Home Colony. In 1866, the house and grounds reverted back to the Destrehans. One of Jean Noel Destrehan's daughters, Louise, and her second husband, Judge Pierre Rost, managed to revive the sugarcane operation. Yet, the end of an era was near. On Louise's death in 1877, her son Emile tried his hand at managing the complex, but poor health hampered his good intentions. Emile sold Destrehan Plantation in 1910, marking the end of the family's ownership of Destrehan Manor, and its status as a leading producer of sugarcane.

All, however, was not lost. Destrehan's enormous size and prime location facing the river appealed to a new industry. An oil refinery sprouted up over the indigo and sugarcane fields; the manor house itself functioned as an office complex and company headquarters. Destrehan Plantation adapted to the changing times. But in 1958, after 168 years of use, the aging home was deemed obsolete. Hope faded.

For the next thirteen years, she lay vacant. Her derelict condition—boarded windows, broken railings, peeling plaster, exposed bricks—cast a depressing pall over the area.

In *Gumbo Ya-Ya: Folk Tales of Louisiana,* Lyle Saxon insists that such a brooding environment is the perfect breeding ground for haunted tales: "Of course every old plantation home in Louisiana has at least one ghost. Any that did not would sink into the earth in sheer shame, the moment such a fact became known, for a spook is as necessary to a plantation as a legend of family silver buried in the ground by faithful slaves the day the damyankees came."

The River Road Historical Society disputes Saxon's theory; they believe that the plantation's honored legacy is sufficiently appealing without a pirate ghost on board. Behind Destrehan's restored 1839 Greek Revival facade lies a wealth of drama.

Beginning in 1787 Frenchman Robert Antoine Robin de Logny hired a free mulatto named Charles to build a raised house "sixty feet in length by thirty-five feet," with a surrounding gallery, five chimneys, and a hipped roof. Charles labored by hand for three years to complete the project. For his efforts, Robin de Logny paid him "one hundred piastres, fifty quarts of rice and corn, a cow and her calf, and a brute slave." After the payment is recorded, there is no further mention of homebuilder Charles; he must have packed up his earnings and looked for a more lucrative line of work elsewhere.

Owner and planter Robin de Logny didn't last long either. He died in 1792, scarcely having time to enjoy his new home. Robin's son Pierre tried his hand at management, but thought better of it. In 1802, Pierre de Logny turned over the plantation to his new brother-in-law, Jean Noel Destrehan. The marriage of Jean Noel Destrehan to Pierre's sister, Celeste de Logny, joined two of the wealthiest families in the Louisiana colony.

The newlyweds' roles were preordained. Jean Noel would convert the indigo plantation into one of the most profitable sugarcane operations in the South; Celeste would raise the children. Large families were the norm in French Catholic Louisiana. Celeste complied, giving birth to fourteen babies. To make room for the growing family, two matching wings were added to the manor house in 1810.

Evidence of the aristocratic Destrehans' allegiance to their native France remains on display throughout the home. A portrait of Emperor Napoleon Bonaparte hangs in the front parlor, but another less-traditional family memento is the star attraction at this plantation-turned-museum. For favors rendered, the French emperor presented Jean Noel Destrehan with a solid white marble bathtub! The deed that prompted the strange thank-you gift remains a mystery.

As the owner of a prosperous plantation, Jean Noel Destrehan entertained lavishly and furnished his home with the latest fashions from Europe. When the French tricolor was lowered and the American stars and stripes raised, Jean Noel quickly switched gears; well versed in politics, he helped shape Louisiana's new state constitution in 1812.

Downriver in New Orleans things were also looking up for French expatriates Jean Lafitte and his older brother Pierre. From the back of a blacksmith shop on Bourbon Street, they conducted a thriving business selling stolen wares to a wealthy clientele, a clientele who happily circumvented payment of the hefty United States custom tax on imported goods.

By 1813 pirate Jean Lafitte was at the height of his success, operating in open defiance of the United States government. Biographer Saxon writes, "Weekly deliveries of contraband goods still came to New Orleans and convoys of sailing boats and swift pirogues went each week through Bayou Lafourche to the rich plantations along its banks." Door-to-door, or at least dock-to-dock, deliveries from the bayous to the river were readily available. Orders for "Black Ivory" (slaves) were filled with increasing regularity.

Destrehan docent Marion Hebert is positive the honorable patriarch, Jean Noel Destrehan, would never have stooped to dealing in such illicit trade. "Here's a man who's putting together the state constitution and believes in the laws that he's writing." If paragon of virtue Jean Noel was not in on any pirate scheme, then, reasoned the treasure hunters, some other family member, unencumbered by legal or ethical technicalities, must have been in contact with the pirate; why else would Jean Lafitte's ghost haunt this plantation?

Destrehan family papers hint at several candidates. In his final will, written in New Orleans on April 22, 1818, Jean Noel Destrehan beseeches his wife, Celeste de Logny, to exert the utmost caution in supervising their nine surviving children. "If my son, Jean Etienne, continues to give himself to drink and to conduct himself badly, I implore my wife and the trustee of my younger children to instigate an interdiction against him."

It appeared that Jean Etienne was traveling in questionable circles and was in danger of losing his inheritance. Writing in *Le Communiqué*, the newsletter of the River Road Historical Society, editor Irene Tastet is hopeful that future research will provide answers on whether or not Jean Etienne Destrehan mended his ways. Bad boy or not, there is no substantial proof that Jean Etienne hooked up with any pirate—or provided a safe haven for Jean Lafitte to stash his loot.

Marion Hebert believes that the entire story of a finger-pointing ghost is a case of mistaken identity. For her, the missing link between the perfidious pirate and the plantation was neither patriarch Jean Noel nor his excommunicated son Jean Etienne, but rather Jean Etienne's brother, Nicholas Noel Destrehan. Gazing fondly at an oval portrait of the handsome Nicholas on display in the bedroom, Marion explains that in the early 1800s boys were considered men at fourteen. No longer allowed to live in the main house, they either moved into separate quarters known as *garçonnières* or were given a plantation of their own to manage. Young Nicholas chose to set up housekeeping on family lands on the west bank of the river below Destrehan, placing him in proximity to a well-traveled route of Lafitte's band of pirates, the Baratarians.

Like a mother with a wayward child, Marion is indulgent when it comes to Nicholas. She believes that the exciting exploits of the pirate were irresistible to a young boy. "Jean Lafitte would come up Barataria [Bay] and Nicholas' plantation was right there. . . . Nicholas probably admired him, you know, a dashing man. They became friends and Jean Lafitte would stop at Nicholas' plantation and visit with him."

Compounding the confusion over names, Nicholas's father's plantation on the east bank of the river and Nicholas's own on the west bank were both called Destrehan. Jean Lafitte, Jean Noel, Jean Etienne, Nicholas Noel; Destrehan on the east bank, Destrehan on the west bank; stormy night, winding river—any ghost might get a bit confused after being on the prowl for nearly two centuries.

Acquiescing momentarily to the popular notion of a phantom pirate on the grounds, docent Hebert allows that *if* Jean Lafitte's ghost popped up at Destrehan Plantation (on the east bank; son Nicholas Noel's plantation on the west bank no longer exists), he probably just lost his bearings and wound up pointing to the wrong house, on the wrong side of the river (navigation on foggy nights can be tricky and spirits occasionally are blown off course). Under such trying circumstances, the ghost of Jean Lafitte can't possibly be held accountable if foolish mortals choose to follow him.

Contrary to the official policy of the River Road Historical Society, stories of the pirate and his treasure flourish. Adjusting the silk ribbons on her bonnet, docent Hebert admits it's difficult; visitors hear the rumors. "They're interested. Ghosts hold a fascination for most people. They ask about hauntings, and they'll say, 'I really want to see something.'" Unwittingly, Marion Hebert's solid-black Creole mourning outfit—hat, veil, gloves, dress—lends itself all too well to tales of the supernatural. Marion is dressed in character as one of the Destrehan wives who lost her husband at a young age. Marion's personal position on ghosts does veer a bit from the party line. "For a house to survive as long as this one, or any old buildings, they're going to have an essence, you know. We carry something with us, whether it's good or whether it's sad. It stays behind for a little time. I think that's what this house is filled with, the essence of many, many people." When pressed to identify a few of these entities, Marion confesses, "I am drawn to Nicholas. That's the simplest way I can put it. There's something about him that touches my heart and saddens me. I read a lot about Nicholas. He married at the age of twenty-one to a girl named Victoire Fortier. He loved her dearly. They were married for eleven years when she died. Nicholas mourned her for the rest of his life. He married again and had a family with his second wife, but he requested to be buried with Victoire in the cemetery of the Red Church up the road. On the tomb he says how much he loved her and that he would meet her again in the afterlife."

A deep sigh escapes from Marion. "Sometimes it's almost like I can feel Nicholas, his presence, his sadness." As for the ghost of the finger-pointing pirate Jean Lafitte and his treasure, Ms. Hebert shakes her head, smiles, and lowers her veil.

6

The Ghost and
the Real Scarlett O'Hara

With her etch-a-sketch coastline battered by pugnacious storms from the Gulf, "trembling prairies" of vast watery-marshlands, and a café-au-lait river looping back on itself, time and place in the lands of Louisiana are freeform, an abstract painting in progress. Leaving their imprints on this flowing canvas were a lively young couple—and another conniving pirate.

They were Felicité and Hypolite Chretien. The pirate was a cohort of Jean Lafitte. He wanted her gold and jewels. She whipped out a pistol and shot him dead. Their encounter was recreated in the epic movie *Gone with the Wind.* The stairwell of Chretien Point Plantation served as the model for the Hollywood movie set where Scarlett O'Hara shot the "damyankee" as he tried to grab her mama's sewing basket.

In the real-life version at Chretien Point Plantation, after the outmaneuvered pirate collapsed in a pool of blood, his body was stashed in a secret compartment under the stairs. Current owner Louis Cornay believes that the pirate—his spirit, not his crumbling bones—may be with them still. Juggling past and present, the Cornays have adapted to the occasional tinkering of their ghostly housemate, although sharing living quarters with the ghost they call "Robert" has required a few adjustments.

When Louis Cornay, an interior designer, and his wife, Jeanne, a professor of English, first saw the antebellum marvel known as Chretien Point Plantation near Opelousas, they were enthralled. With its fan-shaped lunettes over the windows reminiscent of the Palace of Versailles, and Tuscan columns soaring to meet a gray slate roof, the magnificence of the home was evident, even when cloaked in cobwebs. Digging into the plantation's long history, Louis and Jeanne were soon convinced that, scene for scene, the saga of Chretien Point was surely deserving of an Oscar for "Best Screenplay Based on Original Material."

The first owners, Hypolite and Felicité Chretien, were a passionate and peculiar couple. Their antics rivaled those of the fictional characters in Margaret Mitchell's sweeping *Gone with the Wind* drama. Certainly the feisty Felicité Neda Chretien would have had little trouble upstaging the indomitable Scarlett O'Hara. Dispensing with the myth of the swooning Southern belle, Louis Cornay holds out his right hand and, with thumb tapping each finger in turn, methodically ticks off the extraordinary habits of Felicité: "She rode her horse astride like a man instead of sidesaddle like a lady was supposed to; she wore trousers instead of a skirt; she went tearing through the countryside; she smoked cigars; and she gambled." Glancing at Felicité's gilt-framed portrait adorning the mantel in the dining hall, the charming Mr. Cornay is clearly infatuated with the former lady of the manor. "Scarlett O'Hara actually had the same personality as our wonderful Felicité, *except* Felicité was a real person. She was absolutely the first liberated woman in Louisiana!"

Continuing the comparison between the two ravishing beauties, Louis Cornay comments on their effect on the opposite sex. "All the young men wanted to marry Felicité, and they courted her, just like in the movie everybody was courting Scarlett, but only one guy was smart enough to make the right offer." The impeccably groomed Mr. Cornay nods in obvious pleasure at the cunning of the "one guy" who won the hand of the untamed Felicité.

With an enticing game-show-host flourish, Louis Cornay reveals Felicité's unorthodox marriage proposal. "He was Hypolite Chretien II. He offers Felicité Neda, daughter of a Spanish nobleman, a *reverse* dowry to marry him." The usual custom, explains Cornay, called for the expectant bride's father to negotiate with various suitors until an acceptable dowry was proffered to the prospective groom. The smitten Hypolite bypassed tradition, *and* the other suitors in line, striking a bargain directly with Felicité. His inducement, according to Cornay, was "a bribe . . . the equivalent of over fifty thousand dollars in today's money!" Like the resourceful Scarlett, Felicité eyed the cash and hooked up with Hypolite. And like that of their fictional counterparts, Scarlett and Rhett, the colorful marriage of Felicité and Hypolite skirted the norm of the day. The Chretiens, husband and wife, were also daring entrepreneurs, filling the family coffers with profits from cotton and *contraband.*

Louis Cornay continues his tale of the Chretiens' foray into the black market, jumpstarting it with a fanciful encounter at the Battle of New Orleans. On January 8, 1815, Gen. Andrew Jackson assembled a mixed bag of fighting men to defend the city and defeat the British. Hypolite, still just an adventurous teenager, traveled south with a few fellow planters and signed up with Jackson's troops near Chalmette.

Waving his arms to represent the colliding American and British forces, Louis Cornay whips up a scene in the gory battle: "Hypolite is crouched in a ditch with his uncle. A guy on the American side runs in front of them. The guy takes a hit in his leg and falls. The young Hypolite crawls from the safety of the ditch—everybody's brave when they're eighteen. Hypolite drags the guy to safety, tends his wound, and gets him ready to go again. The fellow says, 'Thank you very much.' They introduce themselves and the young fellow says he's Hypolite Chretien, and the other guy says, 'My name is Jean Lafitte.'" Of course, says an excited Cornay, it's the pirate!

Biographer Lyle Saxon writes that Jean Lafitte and his gang, the Baratarians, had an ulterior motive siding with the

Americans in the battle for control of New Orleans. They hoped to ease the mounting opposition to their illegal activities and gain favor as loyal patriots to the American cause. After the American victory, the young Hypolite returned to Opelousas to oversee his cotton crops, and the pirates enjoyed their fifteen minutes of fame. With the stroke of a feathered pen, the "hellish banditti" were reborn in Gen. Andrew Jackson's reports to Pres. James Madison as "privateers" (authorized bounty hunters), and their sins were forgiven. But the honeymoon was short. The dual mantle of model citizen/loyal patriot was an uncomfortable fit for Jean Lafitte and his merry men. The genteel citizenry of La Nouvelle-Orléans still refused to invite the pirates to dine with their wives and daughters. Incensed, Lafitte pulled up stakes and moved his band of Baratarians beyond the reach of the United States territorial authorities. He used Galveston Island, then part of the Republic of Texas, as his new base of operations.

Lafitte realized he still needed a place to sell his stolen wares to the prosperous Creole planters back in Louisiana. A solution, says Louis Cornay, was within reach. "The best thing Lafitte can figure out is to come and see his friend [Hypolite Chretien] in Opelousas, west of New Orleans. Hypolite would bring his friends here to the land he owns at Chretien Point and the pirates would bring their goods inland across the prairies of southwest Louisiana in wagons. They'd buy and sell right here."

Hypolite and Felicité's "garden parties" must have been a strange sight indeed: giant open-air garage sales held under swaying oak, cherry, pecan, and tallow trees. Proper Creole gentlemen in top hats, canes, and polished boots mingled with scruffy seamen clutching in callused hands a dowager's emerald brooch, a filigreed Celtic cross, or a diamond-encrusted tiara. The net result, according to Louis Cornay, was a mutually beneficial association. "Of course, the pirates would take their share and put it in their pockets and go away, and Hypolite would take his share, put it in his pockets, and get richer and richer and richer."

With their share of the profits, Hypolite and Felicité built a grand home in 1831 on the Coteau Ridge, overlooking Bayou Bourbeau. Besides hosting regular sales of contraband on the grounds, Chretien Point Plantation served as the center of a thriving 10,000-acre cotton operation. The fairytale life was in full bloom when Hypolite was bitten by a mosquito carrying the insidious yellow fever, and he died. Bravely Felicité stepped right in, keeping the pirate trade rolling. The astute Felicité dug up Hypolite's stash of gold buried on the grounds (Hypolite did not believe in banks) and doubled her husband's fortune (some say via many a winning poker hand).

There are numerous theories about what happened to the Baratarians, but by the late 1830s only a small disorganized band of pirates was left operating out of Galveston Island. Cornay says the gang realized it was time to move on. "The last ones needed money, as all good pirates are always broke, and they decided to make one last run into Louisiana."

The pirates' scheme called for plunder and—murder. Their target was the wealthy widow, Felicité Chretien. Cornay wipes his glasses with a crisp, white-linen handkerchief and lowers his voice in the best storytelling tradition. "The pirates came here one night. There were seven left of Lafitte's gang, darting in and out of the trees." Cornay pauses for effect, turning his head towards the French doors. "Felicité is putting the children to bed and happens to hear a horse neigh in the front yard. She looks out and sees dark figures approaching. She goes to her dresser, opens the drawer, and grabs a handful of jewels and a pistol."

Pointing to the upper landing of the stairwell, Cornay draws a frightening picture. "Felicité is standing at the head of the stairs waiting . . . for sure, one of the pirates comes in the door and starts inching up the steps. With a single candle flickering like a spotlight behind her, Felicité rattles her jewelry, gasps, and orders the pirate not to come any further." Cornay smugly emphasizes that "Felicité was very smart—what she was really saying was 'Come a little closer; I can't see you well enough yet.'"

Lured by the glittering jewels, the greedy pirate placed a muddy boot on the second ramp of steps. Felicité pulled the pistol out from behind her back and shot him dead. The unlucky pirate fell on the eleventh step.

In Louis Cornay's rendition of the events, Felicité jumped over the dead Baratarian, called for her servants, gave them rifles, and chased the rest of the gang away. The house servants took the body and hid it in the cabinet under the stairs. They scrubbed the blood from the carpet, but neglected to wash the wood underneath. This stain provided the Cornays with their first clue to the identity of the ghost haunting Chretien Point Plantation.

Over the years, Chretien Point, like so many other plantations, fell into disrepair. The vacant mansion was used by local farmers. Hay was stored in its rooms. Cows, chickens, and pigs made themselves at home. When Louis and Jeanne Cornay arrived in 1975, they had to push out many a stubborn farm animal. "When we were cleaning up, I noticed this really dark, almost black stain, on the eleventh step. Not knowing what it was, we tried to bleach it out, but by the time we had completed the remainder of the restoration, we had given up." Cornay is now glad his attempts to remove the stain were unsuccessful.

A few months after moving in, the Cornays learned of a man who had been born in the house in 1890 and was living in Port Arthur, Texas. They invited him to come and see what he thought of their restoration efforts. "One evening this ninety-year-old man and his wife come tearing up the driveway. He drove himself," says Louis Cornay in amazement. "It was quite a sight. Birds were flying out of the way, dust was blowing, and he came charging up to the house. He was a little bitty fella, barely 5'4", and he says, 'I'm Tumpy Chretien and I've come to see *my* house!'" Cornay interrupts his own story. "Now, Hamilton ("Tumpy") Chretien hasn't been here since the turn of the century, so we bring him in to show him around, and after his first sentence I realize he is going to show us around!"

Louis and Jeanne Cornay followed the crotchety figure to the stairwell, where he proceeded (like the long-dead pirate) to move slowly and deliberately up the steps to the first landing. Stopping abruptly at step number eleven, Tumpy Chretien looked down and announced to the startled Cornays that the bloodstain was still there! The ensuing conversation between Louis Cornay and the elderly Mr. Chretien was a bit contentious.

Responding to Mr. Chretien's identification of the mark, a puzzled Louis Cornay questioned his reference to *The Bloodstain*.

The aged visitor squinted at Louis Cornay and tersely gave a one-syllable reply. "Yes!"

Cornay countered, "How do you know that's a bloodstain?"

The exasperated Tumpy Chretien grabbed Cornay's arm, spitting out, "My granddaddy told me it's a bloodstain."

Unconvinced, Louis pressed on. "Well, how did your grand-daddy know it was a bloodstain?"

Stretching his bent frame upwards to look Louis in the eye, Mr. Chretien inhaled a raspy breath, then blew out his final answer. "Because my granddaddy was one of the children in the house the night of the killing, and he told me what Felicité did to save them!"

The episode with the elderly Tumpy Chretien confirmed for Louis Cornay the identity of the ghost who plays devilish tricks to make his point. This is a ghost, believes Cornay, without a sense of humor, a ghost who insists on a little respect.

One of the first signs of a ghostly presence occurred shortly after Cornay opened the home to tours. "One night a bus company asked if they could have a nighttime tour. I allowed them to come and told the story about the guy on the stairs. I sort of laughed up my sleeve." Louis lets out a few staccato "ha-ha-ha" sounds, imitating himself. That evening after making fun of the idea of a ghost in the house, Louis says he began to believe that perhaps the spirit of the slain pirate was indeed hanging around. Cornay was awakened at five o'clock the next morning by the unrelenting bleating of his car horn. He went outside and was about to unplug the wires to disconnect the horn when, instead, for reasons he cannot explain, he reached in the window and passed his hand across the steering wheel. "I ran my hand over it without touching it, sort of like the way you might push someone's hand out of the way, and the horn stopped just like that." Louis snaps his fingers in the air. With the noise gone, Louis went back to bed, but an hour later, the honking resumed. This time, says Cornay, he knew just what to do. "I went outside and ran my hand across the horn pad, pushing the invisible hand away, and the horn stopped."

A few nights later, Cornay relates, he and his wife were hosting a family dinner party and he began talking about the strange occurrences with the car horn. Everyone found the story amusing except for Cornay's cousin, who became quite agitated. Louis firmly told his cousin that the events really did happen exactly as he said. Pounding both hands on the table in outrage, Louis's cousin declared Louis to be crazy—"Ghosts can't make things happen!" Just then the two front doors in the dining room flew open. "They were latched," confirms the present owner, "just like they are latched now."

Several months passed. Louis Cornay put the incidents behind him. As he led another evening tour through rooms decorated with period antiques—mahogany armoires, silk-draped beds, French walnut tables on cabriole legs—Cornay decided to entertain the group with a lighthearted tale of their touchy ghost. He went on at length describing the foolish pirate who fell for Felicitié's ruse. Again at precisely five the next morning, the horn on his car began a persistent blaring. Stumbling out of bed, Louis Cornay descended the stairs—making careful note of step eleven—opened the car door, waved his hand over the steering wheel, and the horn stopped.

The practical Mr. Cornay no longer pokes fun at his pirate ghost, preferring to avoid the irritating wakeup call. Louis offers a simple rationale. "The guy was saying don't make fun of me and everything is okay."

Cornay now treads lightly when it comes to supernatural

phenomena. "When we first moved into the home, I was skeptical of what you use the word ghost for, and I have decided that instead of ghost, it's energy sources left by people who lived here before. As long as you are respectful of this energy that is in the house, it isn't evil, and it isn't bad or anything—it's just that we're all living here together."

Realizing the marketing potential of this melding of past and present, Chretien Point Plantation hosts "Candlelit Ghost Dinners," where guests are invited to "arrive at dusk, drive through centuries-old oaks dripping with Spanish moss," and as the candles flicker "listen to the legends of Felicité, Hypolite, Jean Lafitte—and 'Robert,'" the name the Cornays have given to the errant pirate who met his end at the hands of a valiant damsel.

7

Murder, Mystery, and Mayhem at Loyd Hall

A forlorn Union suitor plays the violin on the upper gallery and entertains children in the attic; a cantankerous poltergeist swipes silverware from the table. The spirits of Loyd Hall in Cheneyville stake out their territory, yet owner Anne Fitzgerald is unfazed. Sitting on the Victorian settee in the front parlor, Mrs. Fitzgerald extends the same cordial welcome to former occupants as she does to overnight guests, who come to savor antebellum life in all its varied forms. Anne Fitzgerald is proud of Loyd Hall's haunted lineup. With her pale-red hair glinting in the sunlight, she declares in an inviting drawl, "We have wonderful ghosts and spirits with us."

Resident tour guide Beulah Davis, a strikingly tall black woman, bolstered by a proud, ramrod-straight carriage, feels that the hauntings began with William Loyd, the original builder. Standing next to a heavily carved armoire in the master bedroom, the regal Beulah speaks of the red-bearded William as if he has just breezed through the keyhole-framed doorway. "I feel his presence here. He is somewhat of a mysterious-type person."

Anne Fitzgerald supports Beulah's account, noting that William Loyd was accused of being both a Union and a

Confederate sympathizer, and wound up "tarred, feathered, and hung from one of the large oaks in the front yard."

In a clipped cadence, Beulah elaborates. "During the Civil War between the Union and the Confederate soldiers, they occupied Loyd Hall at different times. The Unions had taken it as a command post, and the Confederates were camped out in the woodside. William Loyd was caught like a double spy between the two, kind of playing them off, one against the other. I think he's still here today trying to do the same to family members and guests and animals." With unswerving conviction, Beulah expresses her faith in William's supernatural abilities. "He comes in all types of forms at Loyd Hall."

Spirit possession is a tenet of many spiritual churches in the African-American community, especially in the Deep South. For a brief moment, Beulah Davis cracks open the door to her childhood, speaking guardedly of her parents and their belief that souls of the dead can take on many shapes and disguises. "They always told us ghost stories at night when we were sitting around the fire before we'd go to bed. Sometimes they'd have us so fired up we wouldn't be able to sleep."

In her thought-provoking study, *Night Riders in Black Folk History,* author Gladys-Marie Fry tracks ghost stories passed on from slave ancestors—scary tales with sinister undercurrents. "If slaves could not be sufficiently frightened with things of this earth, one other recourse was open to the masters and overseers—fear of the supernatural, primarily ghosts . . . the master, for all his power, was only flesh and blood and bones; the ghost was not subject to such limitations." Fry purports that during the plantation era in the decades prior to the Civil War there was "a systematic exploitation of black folk beliefs and fears." The slightest hint of a ghost lurking about was a "dominant factor employed by wealthy planters to control slave movements."

Beulah Davis agrees. "They always would try to keep 'em within their own plantation . . . so they wouldn't be influenced about what was going on at the other particular plantations. They [the white masters] could keep rein over 'em. They didn't allow them to visit one another, even if it was family. They weren't allowed to go to the next plantation because . . . they didn't want them [the slaves] to start an uprising over the owners."

Ms. Fry's research asserts that ghost stories fuel the belief that spirits of the dead do not rest and can return under the guise of supernatural monsters. In Beulah Davis's family, deceased relatives often came back if there was "trouble in the family or someone was real sick." Ms. Davis's parents believed that the souls of her grandparents could appear in animal form. "They said they've been walking along the road at night, coming home, and they'd see a white figure and it'll be a little dog or cat and when they got to the end, it disappears like it was never there."

Not surprisingly, Beulah Davis sees nothing strange with the long-deceased William Loyd's own penchant for returning in the phantom shape of a large white dog. If William did indeed spend a lifetime as an expert in subterfuge, then perhaps it is not such a stretch to imagine his soul materializing as a shaggy four-legged creature. Ms. Davis believes that William Loyd's spirit is so persistent because "he really didn't get to finish what he started with this beautiful old house."

Loyd Hall's other ghosts also favor the occasional disguise. "Sometimes it looks like a man and sometimes it looks like a woman; sometimes it may be just a silhouette or a white oval shape." The choice, says the fair-minded Ms. Davis, is arbitrary.

Beulah's first paranormal experiences at this 640-acre working plantation were of the benign variety: muffled footsteps, doors opening and closing, objects moving about. Initially Beulah chalked it up to her imagination. "My parents always told me about visions they had, but until I came to Loyd Hall, I never really truly experienced anything like that." Through the years, as Beulah worked at Loyd Hall, her opinion changed. "In certain rooms when you can see a figure or a shape moving on your side vision, and you know you're the only person that's supposed to be there that's alive, when you

kind of catch it, that's when I decided that there was something for real." To the doubters Beulah cautions, "Wait until
you have that personal experience and then you decide!"

Floating through the night air thick with the smell of jasmine and gardenia, the first haunting note heard by many
guests at Loyd Hall is from a melancholy violin solo by the
"Midnight Pied Piper." Surprisingly the tune is not produced
by the multitalented William Loyd, a.k.a. "Wily Willie," a.k.a.
"The Doggone Trickster." Rather, the ghostly sonata is attributed to one Harry Henry.

Beulah Davis describes Harry as a young Union soldier who
just decided to stay behind and desert his regiment. Anne
Fitzgerald indicates there was more than a little incentive for
Harry's desertion. "When the Union forces occupied Loyd
Hall, Harry became enamored of the attractive niece of the
family trapped in the house." According to Mrs. Fitzgerald,
when the Union forces pulled out, the lovestruck Harry
elected to stay behind and hide in the attic. Wavering between
laughter and pity, Anne Fitzgerald recounts the sad twist of fate
awaiting the ardent suitor. "Apparently no one informed
Grandmother Loyd that Harry was hiding upstairs. Startled at
bumping into him, she shot and killed him."

In Beulah's version, Grandmother Loyd and Harry struggle
over the gun; the gun goes off and Harry dies. Both Anne and
Beulah agree that Harry was buried in a shallow grave under
the house, and it is Harry's footsteps that are heard coming
down from the attic and crossing onto the balcony, where he
commences to play his sad song on the violin. The ghost of
hapless Harry strokes his first note at midnight.

When Anne and Frank Fitzgerald first moved into the home
that had been renovated by his parents, they, like Teeta Moss
and her husband at The Myrtles Plantation in St. Francisville,
were concerned about the effect of ghosts and apparitions on
their children. Anne explains the situation: "We had three little
girls; they were two, five, and nine. It was one thing for them to
have visited with their grandmother at Loyd Hall, but quite

another for them to live here, go upstairs to bed each evening, and," emphasizes Anne, "I didn't want them to be afraid."

Exercising a mother's prerogative, Anne chose not to talk about ghosts with her daughters, preferring to deal with the haunting issue if, and when, it came up. It arose sooner than expected, and when it did Anne opted for a nonchalant approach.

"I was cooking dinner when I overheard this conversation between the nine year-old and the five-year-old. The nine-year-old said to Melinda: 'What did Harry say today, and what did you and Harry do today?'

"And I'm thinking, *There is no one who works with us here by the name of Harry; we have no relative by the name of Harry; so who is Harry?* Finally I couldn't stand it. I said, 'Girls, who is this Harry we're talking about?'

"They looked at me as if I'd grown two heads and said: 'Mama, Harry is our ghost. He lives on the third floor and plays with us. He's such fun!'"

"Aren't we lucky!" was Anne's quick retort as she went back to stirring the gravy. Her reasoning for not challenging the girls' story was that they were obviously not afraid, and nothing ever occurred to make her uneasy. "Whether it was their active imaginations, or whether Harry had truly joined them, it was a good thing. So we just let them have their fun."

Looking back on her childhood, Melinda Fitzgerald Anderson, now Loyd Hall's manager, has fond memories of her unusual companion. "For years my sister Paige and I had a playmate who was tall, dark, and dressed in a Union uniform. He was like a big brother to us . . . he was the nicest person."

In hindsight, with the Fitzgerald girls grown and with children of their own, Anne does not regret her decision to let her daughters play with a ghost. "It's interesting," reflects Anne. "When we discuss Harry, and I ask them when they first became aware, as children, of the spirit of Harry on the third floor, they'll pause a moment and just say, 'He was always there.' So we take it at that—he just made himself known to them."

Harry continues to make himself known to visitors through his ethereal music, and on rare occasions books himself for a fragmented appearance in the family room. Gesturing to the back of the double parlor, Anne Fitzgerald describes one of these peculiar sightings. "One of the ladies was doing some cleaning in our family room and she felt something. Looking down she saw a pair of shiny black boots and the tip end of a saber as though it was a sword by his side." Anne immediately questioned the woman, seeking a more detailed description of what the "soldier" actually looked like. Shaken, the woman refused to look further and would only repeat over and over: "I just kept cleanin', just kept cleanin'."

Loyd Hall is an equal-opportunity haven for ghosts. Two female spirits also favor the hassle-free accommodations offered by the current owners. Anne Fitzgerald identifies one as a former nanny wearing "a long black dress with draped sleeves, white apron, and a turban on her faceless head." A visiting psychic determined that when the ghost was ready to reveal herself more fully, she would.

Beulah Davis needs no introduction to this ghost. "Her name is Sally. She was a black slave nanny that lived in the house with the family, but died very mysteriously. They think she might have been poisoned." Beulah swears "Sally" appears during the day in the same room with the boot-and-sword, half-figure apparition of Harry. "I don't know what that room holds for her," admits Beulah, "but on the mantel it is very odd; you cannot keep tall tapered candles standing. We always find 'em lying on the floor. Any other place, any other mantel in the house, they'll stay put."

Anne Fitzgerald says the nanny is also seen in an upstairs bedroom formerly used as a nursery. Today it holds a cradle, and a large four-poster bed with a trio of cloth dolls napping peacefully on an embroidered pillow.

The other known female spirit residing in this circa-1820 Federal-Georgian manor is the victim of unrequited love. Anne Loyd was a niece of William Loyd—a different niece from the one who caused the hapless Harry to desert his regiment. There are no records of what became of niece number one. By contrast, Anne Loyd's death is well documented. Anne was engaged to be married, but her fickle fiancé changed his mind and ran off. The dejected Anne committed suicide by throwing herself out of the third-floor window.

After an unsolicited inspection of the house, the same visiting psychic decreed that the third floor of Loyd Hall contained a high concentration of paranormal activity—not that Beulah Davis or Anne Fitzgerald needed any validation of their ghosts. The psychic also designated the master bedroom on the second floor as the most likely spot to hear footsteps. Anne Fitzgerald allows that this is within the realm of possibilities, as this is the room where William Loyd was placed under house arrest by the Union soldiers before his execution. "I believe that it is him pacing back and forth, not knowing exactly when his demise was going to come, and he was pondering his future."

Undaunted by their tragic fates, the spirits of Loyd Hall rarely brood. Rather, they seem to possess a certain playfulness. Beulah Davis reports that the ghostly antics are just "their small way of letting you know they're here." The tolerant tour guide just wishes they wouldn't move things quite so far. "They change things around. You would at least expect to find it in the same room; instead it's in a totally different part of the house." Snatching knives, forks, and spoons is a favorite prank. "We can set the dining room for lunch or dinner and there's not a time we can sit down that there's not silverware missing. Napkins, glasses, we'll find in other rooms in the house."

Phillip J. Jones, secretary of the Louisiana Department of Culture, Recreation, and Tourism, lends credence to the stories of moving objects. "There's a wonderful bed and breakfast in the central part of the state called Loyd Hall and we were there having a dinner."

Ms. Davis recalls his visit. "He [Phillip Jones] was sitting at the long dining-room table at the end. They had totally moved his silverware. It was there as he sat down, but as he started to eat his food, he found several pieces missing. He called it to my attention, and that's when I told him, 'I told you the ghosts do exist here.'"

After dinner, the group retired to the front parlor. State official Phillip Jones has no easy explanation for the evening's events. "We were listening to the curator [Beulah Davis], who has been in the home giving tours for some twenty years. She said one of the things the ghosts apparently like to do is topple the candlesticks, and as we were sitting there discussing this, one of the candlesticks just came out of its silver holder and fell to the wooden floor." Jones' evaluation of the situation is forthright. "I realized there probably is a little bit of truth to the fact that this home is haunted." The youthful-looking Jones also confesses, "I was a little skeptical at first, you know, but it's a true story. It really is."

Anne Fitzgerald says the tendency of Loyd Hall's ghosts to move objects about is actually an asset. "Our ghosts are wonderful because they do things which save us an embarrassment sometimes. If we have failed to do something or something is out of place, we can always say, 'Well, our ghosts did that, you know—they must have been very active last night.'"

Beulah Davis seconds Anne Fitzgerald's enthusiastic endorsement of the ghosts of Loyd Hall. "We feel like it's a good thing, 'cause we feel like that they're still here in some way, and that they truly watch over this property, I think, and give it an ambiance of its own."

The house itself is a tale of hidden treasure. "One of the real interesting points about this house," declares an amazed Anne Fitzgerald, "is, first of all, my in-laws bought the property without knowing the house was here." Built in the early 1800s, the house was dubbed "Loyd's Folly" due to its mismatched Georgian/Greek Revival architecture and relative isolation on Bayou Boeuf. Piecing together its early history, Anne Fitzgerald refers to one theory that holds that William Loyd was the proverbial black sheep of the prominent Lloyd family of England. The disgraced William was forced to alter his surname, dropping one of the *l*s. William Lloyd was born again as William Loyd. Leaving England, he arrived in Tennessee, then headed southward to create a thinly disguised branch of the Lloyd family tree in Louisiana. William Loyd enjoyed a modicum of success until he reverted to some bad habits, playing the "double-agent" game during the Civil War.

After William's hanging at the hands of the Union forces, "Loyd's Folly" was left to William's brother James and remained in the Loyd family until 1871. For the next seventy-one years, Loyd Hall was a victim of bad gambling debts and bad planning. While the fertile soil of the surrounding acreage continued to be tilled and planted with an assortment of crops—cotton, corn, and soybeans—the maintenance of such a large house was beyond the means of the straggling parade of twenty-one unlucky owners. Left exposed to the elements, "Loyd's Folly" fell into such disrepair that it wasn't even listed on legal deeds.

When Anne's in-laws purchased the six hundred plus acres in 1948 to pasture their herd of cattle, no one bothered to tell them there was a house on the property. The senior Fitzgeralds didn't discover they owned an antebellum home, a haunted one at that, until they came out to fence in the herd.

"Two and a half stories, four chimneys, ten rooms [and assorted ghosts]—so overgrown," explains Anne, "you couldn't see it from the road." Another unexpected sweet bonus was 200 pounds of honey dripping from the balcony, courtesy of a thriving colony of bees. Tunneling through years of accumulated debris inside the house, the Fitzgeralds were rewarded by the sight of a suspended staircase fashioned of tiger maple, mahogany, and walnut, intricate ceiling friezes and medallions, hand-carved cypress woodwork, and pine flooring.

Today, visitors to this charming country retreat can enjoy a stay in antique-filled cabins or stroll about a working farm. Horses, chickens, local Catahoula hounds, and Clarence, the donkey, all extend a friendly welcome, a welcome matched only by the resident ghost population.

When asked, Beulah Davis generally recommends nightfall as the most propitious time to bump into one of Loyd Hall's playful spirits. "I feel late evening when the sun is going down, that's probably the time of day they'd have been out working . . . they'd be coming in for the day. So I feel as the shadows falls across the house, late evening, that's when you experience things."

Beulah backs up her tip with one final bit of proof: "I've had the opportunity to stay late, waiting for bed-and-breakfast guests. I'll be sitting in the back parlor—we have a beeper on the door that beeps to let you know when somebody enters the house when we're here by ourself—and I could hear very clear the door open and close. I get up, walk out into the hall expecting to find my guest standing there, and it's nothing."

Nothing but a friendly spirit returning home to Loyd Hall.

8

The Rising Spirits of Woodland

Few plantations have endured with a tale as turbulent as Woodland. For a time it appeared she would survive only as "The Plantation on a Bottle." Relegated to a label on a whiskey jar, Woodland Plantation on the lower coast below New Orleans teetered on the brink of obscurity. When Foster Creppel came to the rescue of this dilapidated damsel, he uncovered clues pointing to a grand Creole lady—and not-so-subtle hints that the previous occupants were still around.

"Footsteps, the pounding sounded like footsteps," says Foster Creppel. "It was annoying and frustrating at a time when I thought we were doomed forever to live in ruins." To keep a watchful eye on the renovations, Foster camped out in the derelict home. His companions were owls in the attic, alligators in the barrow pit, and a mysterious ghost with a heavy foot.

Woodland Plantation in West Pointe a la Hache was built to last. Floods of biblical proportions, monstrous hurricanes, bootleggers, carpetbaggers, bats and bugs—all left her battered, but unbowed. New owner Foster Creppel is on a mission to restore this proud relic of another era into an appealing country retreat. Paying guests, not ghosts, are Foster's top priority.

Until the Creppels took over in 1997, Woodland Plantation

was a forgotten smudge, a blur, along the main drag from New Orleans down to the mouth of the Mississippi River. Louisiana 23 in Plaquemines Parish is a four-lane rumbling chute through the heart of "Sportsman's Paradise." Mammoth oil rigs crisscrossing the horizon provide a thriving habitat for the deep-water denizens of the Gulf of Mexico and a major lure for big-game fishermen. The drone of cars, pickup trucks, and big rigs rolling south is a constant. With Barataria Bay to the right and the low-slung levee of the Mississippi River to the left, favored pit stops for these fishermen, hunters, and oil-rig workers are Port Sulphur, Empire, Buras, Venice, and Pilot Town. Few, if any, feel the tug of the past. Few, if any, note that this stretch of the river was once lined on both banks with more than 360 plantations—Magnolia, Myrtle Grove, Live Oak, Celeste. Today the voices of all but one are silenced. Woodland, the lone holdout, harbors their stories—a ghostly orchestra of shared memories.

Yankee sea captains William M. Johnson and George Bradish staked their claim to the lower coast back in 1780. Together they established Magnolia Plantation. Theirs was a unique living arrangement. The two men, their wives, and children all resided under one roof. As described in *Green Fields: Two Hundred Years of Louisiana Sugarcane*, the conjoined families shared "a large two-story house with gable ends, a large center hall and columns extending through the two stories in front and rear." Magnolia was the first great plantation to greet visitors arriving through the mouth of the Mississippi. It attracted a host of the famous and the infamous, including, of course, the swaggering pirate Jean Lafitte.

For the captains, life was smooth sailing. A few years after installing their families within Magnolia's white-pillared walls, Johnson and Bradish shared the honor of being designated America's first Chief River Pilots. The industrious Johnson also served as the postmaster at Pilot Town (then known as Balize) and justice of the peace for Plaquemines Parish. In short, Johnson and Bradish were gone a lot. Back at Magnolia

Plantation, domestic bliss began to unravel. As the children grew, the wives argued incessantly over which of their sons would inherit the grand house and surrounding acreage.

To end the feud, William Johnson, Solomon-like, moved his wife, Sarah Rice, and their children into a new home two miles upriver from Magnolia. Smaller in scale, but with a charming elegance, the residence was known simply as "the Johnson home"; as it gained in stature, it was upgraded to Woodland Plantation.

Capt. William Johnson, now well into his seventies, was ready to retire. Making a final journey to his home state of New York, he left Woodland in the care of his four sons. Two of his sons, George and Bradish Johnson, christened before the family feuds, shared the first and last names of William's former business partner, George Bradish.

The anonymous spirit stalking Woodland Plantation today stays in the shadows. Noisy, yet reticent, he cautiously withholds his true identity. While the Creppels are only the third family of record to own Woodland, potential candidates for "the mysterious ghost in residence" are plentiful.

At the time of the captain's death, Woodland was an 11,000-acre working sugarcane plantation, incorporating four slave quarters housing approximately twenty slaves each, a 5,000-square-foot main house, a large sugar mill, a two-story overseer's house, and twenty-four smaller "workers' cabins." It was a small village.

The captain's eldest son, George Washington Johnson, managed the day-to-day operations until his death in 1856. In 1857, Bradish Johnson bought out his brothers' shares in Woodland, becoming the sole owner. Bradish was fond of wearing precision-striped trousers, Prince Albert coats, and black silk hats. A sketch of this proper gentleman would likely include a favorite gold-tipped cane (the better to pound floors with?). If possible, Foster Creppel would have been the first to snatch it away. In Foster's first few months at Woodland, he slept fitfully on a mattress on the first floor. Awakened nightly by fierce pounding overhead, Foster would race up the curved stairwell to be greeted by—silence.

Foster recalls his early tribulations at Woodland, pushing his patience to the edge. "Moving here—everything was in really bad shape. Lots of rats, snakes, rotten wood from the termites. Just the scope of it, I wasn't really ready for it." If the rising spirits of Woodland wanted Foster's undivided attention, they were going to have to take a number and wait their turn.

Years earlier in the spring of 1871, a far more idyllic picture greeted *Harper's Weekly* reporter Ralph Keeler and artist Alfred Waud. Looking out from the upper deck of the steamboat *Alvin,* they were amazed at the wonders before them: "The river was high, and one actually looked down at the countryside . . . we landed at Woodland, one of the plantations of Mr. Bradish Johnson. Woodland must be his favorite for it is his home while in the South."

Keeler's assessment was accurate. Like his father and brother before him, Bradish was passionately devoted to Woodland—a devotion that may linger still. Although he was in effect an absentee landlord, supervising his Plaquemines Parish holdings from the lofty confines of a Fifth Avenue townhouse in New York City, Bradish returned to Woodland religiously each year for the grinding season (sugarcane harvesting). The dapper and diplomatic Bradish also used his dual citizenship (Yankee and Southern Rebel) to safeguard his ancestral home during the Civil War. He persuaded the U.S. provost marshal to set up headquarters at Woodland. The Federal troops left the Southern residence of the Yankee businessman virtually unscathed.

Spared from the destruction and raids suffered by many neighboring plantations, Woodland enjoyed its greatest period of prosperity after the war.

Stepping off the gangplank of the riverboat, artist Alfred Waud grabbed his sketchpad, capturing late-nineteenth-century Woodland at its peak. Golden stalks of sugarcane rippled in the fields; a carriage, drawn by a pair of dappled grays, bore three lovely ladies, parasols raised to protect their delicate skin from the sun; Woodland with its red-tiled roof and windows open to catch the breeze off the river glimmered like a jewel of Southern hospitality. Waud's captivating sketch of Woodland first appeared in the weekly tabloid *Every Saturday* and set off a chain of events still evident at Woodland today.

Lithographers Nathaniel Currier and James Merritt Ives catapulted Woodland into the limelight when they appropriated Waud's charming sketch for their popular *Homes Across the Country* series. Like early travel posters, the fashionable prints featured a representative home from each region of the country. Currier and Ives did a little revamping of the original Waud sketch, reversing it and tossing in some embellishments of their own like a steamboat in the foreground puffing upriver, and another horse-drawn buggy. They even gussied up the plain box columns in the front with ornate Corinthian capitals. The addition of a half-dozen hoop-skirted ladies, escorted by equally elegant gentlemen, strolling arm in arm about the grounds conveyed the message that life along the Mississippi was an endless round of leisurely teas and parties. Woodland Plantation in West Pointe a la Hache became the poster child for the Grand Old South. This image of Woodland's opulent lifestyle caught the marketing eye of the Southern Comfort Corporation.

In the 1880s a Bourbon Street bartender, M. W. Herron, concocted his own masterpiece just a few miles upriver in New Orleans. He named his full-bodied marvel with a hint of sweetness "Southern Comfort," serving the potent drink directly from a whiskey barrel. As with every successful business enterprise, it's all in the packaging, and by 1934 the Southern Comfort Corporation was on the lookout for the perfect picture for their new label to celebrate the end of Prohibition. The Currier and Ives print of Woodland Plantation soon graced every bottle of "Southern Comfort."

In a bizarre twist, just as the label lured millions to savor the smooth spirits of the new "Grand Old Drink of the South,"

Woodland was drowning in a swirling tide of misfortune. Bradish Johnson died in 1897 and Woodland was sold to a Theodore Starks Wilkinson. Wilkinson, also the owner of Myrtle Grove Plantation, downgraded Woodland to a hunting lodge. Campaigning unsuccessfully for governor of Louisiana, the overextended Wilkinson amassed a $19,000 debt. He forked over Woodland to his brother Horace as repayment on a loan.

The 1920s saw Prohibition etch a new face on the American landscape. Now virtually abandoned, Woodland, with her prime location near the mouth of the Mississippi River, was a favorite haven for bootleggers. They camped out in the great upper hall, where the dormer windows, front and back, provided perfect lookouts. When federal agents arrived on the scene, they watched in frustration as the alert bootleggers tossed the evidence into the river.

By the 1940s, a jungle of weeds enveloped the main house, the sugar mill receded into the forest, and vandals made off with whatever they could carry. Her 11,000 acres were parceled and sold off. The ghosts of Woodland's glory days settled in for a long sleep.

Occasionally an ambitious reporter would file a story: "Woodland Plantation: A Shadow of What It Used to Be"; "Woodland Plantation: Life on the Mississippi"; "Plantation in Peril." The articles stirred little interest. Current residents of the lower coast were intent on pursuing oil and mineral rights. Plantations were a blip in the past. And connoisseurs savoring their smooth Southern Comfort cocktails had no inkling that the mysterious plantation appearing on the bottle actually existed. Like Cinderella in tatters, Woodland lost her invitation to the ball.

Over the years, attempts were made to document this last surviving relic of Plaquemines Parish. In 1997 Tulane University professor of architecture Eugene Cizek, with a grant from the Louisiana Department of Culture, Recreation, and Tourism, surveyed the crumbling buildings. Woodland's thirteen heirs, descendants of Horace Wilkinson, were embroiled in a bitter battle of legal title and rights. Under a court-ordered settlement, the Plaquemines Parish Sheriff's Office auctioned Woodland to the highest bidder. The winning bidders, Foster Creppel and his parents, Jacques and Claire, walked away with a piece of Louisiana history.

Renovating Woodland was like prying open a damaged time capsule. Each shovelful of dirt removed, each sagging floorboard uncovered, each rotten timber, threw up much in the way of discouragement. But like avid treasure hunters, the Creppels also rejoiced when Woodland gave up one of her hoarded secrets.

Evidence of William Johnson's haste to separate the feuding wives at Magnolia Plantation is revealed in the construction of Woodland. Interior walls are at odds with the exterior. The exterior is square and true: front and back views boast seven matching cypress columns, five matching dormer windows, and a broad gallery. Foster Creppel also points to "the two large chimneys on both ends of the house," which "act as anchors" for the entire structure. Once the debris was removed, the inside of Woodland revealed a surprisingly helter-skelter floor plan. One window on the first floor is covered and bisected by an interior wall, while another wall slants crookedly to avoid cutting off a second window. Foster Creppel is left to speculate whether William or Sarah was responsible for changing their minds after the house was built, or if they were just in too much of a hurry to get out of Magnolia and quickly threw together some plans.

These elusive tidbits have allowed the Creppels to see the plantation through the eyes of those who knew her best: William and Sarah Johnson and their sons. Knocking down bee, wasp, and termite nests, the Creppels found a broken fragment of a blue stenciled border under the eaves of a second-floor bedroom. Fourteen months of intensive labor later, this same room is proudly rewrapped with a replica blue-ribboned border. Filling in the gaps in the curved mahogany balustrade of the stairway was like connecting the dots to the past. Now a host of ghostly hands can continue their slow descent to the parlor.

With renovations complete, the foot-pounding ghost has ceased his stomp-dance overhead. Perhaps it was just the long-dormant spirit of Captain Johnson, unaccustomed to the racket of construction, or his proper son Bradish, cane in hand, demanding peace and quiet.

The next hurdle for the Creppels may find them dealing with a whole new set of agitated spirits. In an isolated clearing, to the left of the main house as it faces the river, stand the bleached bones of a tin-roofed wooden slave cabin. When artist Waud and correspondent Keeler came to Woodland, they visited these quarters and took particular note of the voodoo rituals practiced by the slaves. "The prevalence of old heathen superstitions among the blacks of this region is something very remarkable . . . if a plantation negro is sick, he firmly believes that some enemy has been practicing the magical art of hiding dried lizards under his house, or in some such way of bringing about his misfortune." Waud and Keeler were unable to fathom how such "mysterious and revolting rites" could exist.

Conversely if Johnson slaves John, Jim, Robert, and Sam were to focus their ghostly eyes through the broken panes at the oddly clad twenty-first-century figures of the Creppel family and their guests, they would be equally stunned. They too would fearfully question what manner of people these are and what strange and powerful gadgets they possess.

Woodland was home to many generations of slave families. A 1941 guide prepared for the state of Louisiana by the Works Progress Administration reports on one Abner Bean, an ex-slave living "in a row of old, two-story brick slave quarters on the former Johnson Plantation, now called Woodland." Abner states he has been granted the right to live on the grounds "free of rent." He recalls "de war" when he was eleven or twelve years old. He was cutting corn when Admiral Farragut's fleet came upriver with guns blazing. The frail elderly gentleman is proud of his humble quarters, and credits fellow slaves Edgar,

Philomene, and Perroux with their sturdy construction. Abner makes no mention of the large iron rings secured to the walls on the second floor or how they were used to chain runaway slaves to prevent their escape. These brick slave quarters were already in existence when William Johnson pieced together parcels of land to form his new plantation of Woodland. William ordered new wooden quarters to be built in the 1840s and reportedly treated his slaves humanely. Eldest son George Washington Johnson's will called for the emancipation of Woodland's slaves and stipulated that his estate pay for their fares back to the colony of Liberia. How many actually went back was not recorded. The brick slave quarters were destroyed by Hurricane Betsy in 1965; only the grass-covered foundations remain.

As he pokes and prods, unearthing Woodland's multilayered history, Foster Creppel finds cryptic messages in shards of pottery, broken bottles, and rusting tools. The grounds of Woodland are a giant archeological dig—the mysteries of the overseer's cabin and the old sugar mill await future exploration.

Foster took a little detour in 1999, unable to resist the lure of another historic building filled to the rafters with life's joys and sorrows. An 1880s country Gothic-style chapel was slated for demolition. The roof was gone, the floorboards were rotten, and the walls in the apartment behind the altar were marred with satanic symbols and pentagrams. But the price was right. All Foster Creppel had to do was move it fourteen miles upriver to Woodland. Undeterred, this diehard preservationist had St. Patrick's Church cut in half, loaded onto two flatbed trucks, and hauled to the site of the old brick slave quarters. At Woodland the deconsecrated chapel was born again as a restaurant aptly named "The Spirits of Woodland." Arched stained-glass windows cast a rainbow of pastel colors over the polished hardwood floors. The former altar is now a bar, where patrons receive their choice of libations in lieu of sermons.

Ghosts of former parishioners drawn to the old parish church of St. Patrick must make a few adjustments. Forgoing the traditional seating in church pews, the spectral congregation must sit in a circle around the new dining-room configuration. They have, at least for now, let the mortal diners enjoy their meals in relative peace.

Combined, the reincarnation of Woodland Plantation as a country inn and the transformation of a rural church to a restaurant preserve a timeless bond with the plantation families and the slaves who once populated the lower coast below New Orleans.

9

A Capitol Ghost

Louisiana's phantoms have a penchant for plantations; favoring spacious digs, they roam in spectral splendor. One capricious soul upped the ante, electing to haunt a medieval fortress that glows at sunset, eerily reminiscent of Count Dracula's beloved castle in Transylvania.

The Old State Capitol in Baton Rouge looms high on a bluff overlooking the murky Mississippi. Its haphazard Gothic-Victorian architecture harks back to the warring ways of feudal lords, vassals, and serfs. Twin turreted towers, crenellated upper battlements, a stained-glass dome festooned with a disorienting array of cobalt-blue, topaz-gold, and blood-red patches—all cast a hypnotic spell. Given Louisiana's propensity for political squabbles and legislative wrangling, the antiquated structure seems well suited, in form and function, to its intended purpose as the seat of state government. The ghost within delights in taunting the staff. Leaving a trail of dusty footprints, he darts through hallowed halls, zipping up and down the spiral staircase. Triggering alarms, he swipes small objects at random. He's known as Pierre, "The Keeper of the Castle." Herein lies the tale of a capitol ghost, the story of a man so obsessed with missing out on his appointed mission in life that he sent his spirit to fill in for him—the ultimate *voter in absentia.*

Pierre Couvillon served as a member of the Louisiana House of Representatives and the Senate from 1834 to 1851. Described in biographical records as a "gargantuan" man standing more than six feet tall with "a body well proportioned to that height," he relied on his powerful, domineering physical attributes to intimidate his opponents. Like all good politicians, Pierre also possessed a flip side, fluidly switching on his "irresistible personality" and "entrancing storytelling ability" to endear himself to family, friends, and constituents. This firebrand with the dual personality vehemently opposed the corrupt banking practices of the day, lobbying vigorously, according to family legends, to protect the interests of the common man.

Accounts differ on the details of Pierre's death and his ensuing haunted appearances at the Old State Capitol. One version has him succumbing to a heart attack in the heat of a passionate speech against corruption during the 1852 legislative session. His inopportune but dramatic demise is the primary reason officials suspect his spirit of causing the disturbances in the building. Phillip J. Jones, secretary of the Louisiana Department of Culture, Recreation, and Tourism, has heard this bit of folklore but states that history does not support this colorful account. "He [Pierre] didn't die in the Old State Capitol, although he did actually have a tremendous fit. He was at his home in Avoyelles Parish and had a heart attack and died."

Historic records verify that two months prior to the start of the 1852 session, while Pierre was at home, he learned that some of his fellow legislators were eliciting financial favors from the banking establishment (at taxpayers' expense); he exploded over their outrageous conduct.

Pierre was laid to rest in Mansura Catholic Cemetery, leaving behind a wife, ten children, and a seat in the Louisiana State Senate. In a 1996 official press release headlined "Gen. Pierre Couvillon's Ghost Believed to Reside at Old State Capitol,"

Louisiana State Archives Assistant Director Lewis Morris suggests that Pierre's obsession with truth and justice may be the reason his spirit made the long journey from his home in Avoyelles Parish back to Baton Rouge. "He was a powerful orator, and he often spoke out against those who used their office and influence to enrich themselves at the expense of those less fortunate." Morris adds, "It was his sincerity for the ordinary man that played a role in his untimely death."

It is also understandable why Pierre's ghost is a tad put out. Having endured the hassle of returning from the dead and trekking back to the capitol building to keep a vigilant eye on his fellow lawmakers, he has a hard time finding them at work. Some may smile ruefully, saying nothing has changed. However, in Pierre's case, the issue is not one of do-nothing politics, but of logistics. Although he has stoically witnessed a litany of dramatic developments at the capitol during his ghostly tenure, including the tragic vote to secede from the Union in 1861 and the seizure of the capitol by Yankee forces in 1862, Pierre struggles to keep up. The ghostly lawmaker had just marked his first decade of haunting his former cronies, when the Union troops put a torch to the state capitol.

For twenty years after the fire (1862-82), the blackened hulk of the capitol building sat lifeless; Louisiana's government went into exile, moving in a gypsy caravan from Baton Rouge to Opelousas to Shreveport to New Orleans. Despite Pierre's pressing need to haunt halls of the old state capitol building, many citizens favored demolition, expressing disdain for the dilapidated structure. Others sought to preserve the historic building and return the capital to Baton Rouge. Samuel Langhorne Clemens (better known as Mark Twain) sided with the former. Clemens spied "this little sham castle" on his epic 1882 journey downriver. Penning his distaste for its awkward medieval appearance, the river pilot-turned-commentator wrote in *Life on the Mississippi:* "It is pathetic enough that a whitewashed castle, with turrets and things . . . should ever have been built in this otherwise honorable place . . . but it is even more pathetic to see this architectural falsehood under-going restoration and perpetualization in our day, when it would have been so easy to let dynamite finish what a charita-ble fire began."

Perhaps Pierre's spectral hand, raised aloft, *was* counted during the tally of *yeas* and *nays* (voting from beyond the grave, cynics claim, is also a time-honored tradition in Louisiana pol-itics), for eventually, after a good deal of wrangling, the preser-vationists won. Architect William Freret began restoration work on the "Castle" in 1882 and the legislators returned to Baton Rouge under Pierre's watchful eye.

But by 1932, Louisiana lawmakers decided the castle's nooks and crannies were simply two crowded; they needed more modern accommodations and voted to move their offices to a new, larger Art Deco structure down the road. This time poor phantom Pierre was left entirely in the lurch. Spirits of the dead do not necessarily return to haunt with all their faculties intact and "can't always go where they want to." Pierre's ghost was dismayed to find he had once again lost track of the law-makers.

For the next six decades the architectural oddity limped along as a meeting space for various civic and cultural groups. The worn-out specter of Pierre faded with the much-maligned "Castle."

Yet the landmark "Castle" was not without supporters. In 1981, a meticulous thirteen-year, $9.25 million restoration was launched. And in 1994 Pierre's beloved capitol building reopened its hand-hewn cypress doors as Louisiana's Center for Political and Governmental History. Today the museum's gleaming interior belies 150 years of scandal, intrigue, impeachment, the occasional fistfight on the floor, and a long line of combative governors topped by the "Kingfish," Huey Long. At its grand opening, some reviewers raved that the refurbished "Castle" took on a "wedding-cake perfect" persona.

All that spit and polish woke the dormant Pierre. Perplexed at the new state of affairs, he vents his frustration on the staff at the "new" Old State Capitol Museum. Mary Louise Prudhomme, director of the complex, says their first hint of a phantom visitor came from a student worker in the museum's gift shop. "She said the door would open and close all by itself—we have these large heavy doors that don't exactly swing in the breeze." Ms. Prudhomme takes the direct approach; she's a Southern-to-the-core, face-things-head-on, *Steel Magnolia* woman. A tailored cherry-red suit sets off her clipped dark-brown hair. "Now, no one," she declares emphatically, "was really frightened. They just knew it was kind of strange. As more of the employees became involved—coming to me and discussing things that happened to them personally—we began to sense that perhaps we did have ghost."

Security guard/guide John Hoover has no doubt that the ghostly campaign of the "lawmaker extraordinaire" is back in high gear. The gun and holster slung on Hoover's hip seem an odd fit for the kindly grandfather figure with his cap of thick, snow-white hair, but he takes his job seriously. Hoover cleverly turns the pesky Pierre's manifestations to his advantage, using tales of the capitol ghost to keep groups of visiting school-children in line. "I tell the kids that something happened one night that changed my ideas about whether we had a ghost in the building or not."

John takes center stage in the expansive Senate Chamber on the second floor. Sunlight streams through the stained-glass Gothic windows, casting a crazy-quilt mosaic over the oak-planked floor. A group of fourth graders sits cross-legged in a lopsided semicircle at John's feet. Security cameras mounted high on brackets scan the room. John Hoover reminds his captive audience that they are under constant surveillance. "I point out that we have forty security cameras in this building and underneath the cameras is a little white box we call a motion detector." John follows this with a little a demonstration. "I'll have a student or maybe one of the teachers walk towards the motion detector that's behind us here, so they can see a little red light come on. I explain to them that the light not only lights up here at that box, but it also lights up down-stairs at the main security board."

Now that John has laid out the parameters for the defense of the building from the invasion of any intruders (mortal or otherwise), he sets the scene for the night in question. The Capitol Museum is open during the day to tour groups and individuals; at night its vaulted rooms, chambers, and gallery spaces are rented out for a variety of functions from wedding receptions to fundraisers. When the building is not in use, John tells the squirming kids, the sophisticated monitoring sys-tem is supervised by a single guard stationed in front of the security board on the first floor.

At this juncture in his story, John gets down to the scary details: It is 10:30 P.M. Night security guard Wanda Lee Porter is on duty and has relieved the day guard. The motion detec-tor under camera #22 lights up on the security board. Camera #22 is positioned on the first floor, aimed at "The Old Governor's Mansion Collection." The display consists of three rooms: a dining room and two bedrooms. All are decorated with period furniture from past governors. As the light blinks on the board, security guard Porter immediately punches up camera #22 on the big screen so she can scan one of the bed-rooms and look at what has set off the motion detector. She sees nothing. She gets on the phone to check in with the guard she has relieved from the day shift. She asks him if he left "any-one in the building" without telling her. His unequivocal response is "No, indeed no."

Wanda punches up camera #22 again, rescanning the bed-room. "I looked high and I looked low—still nobody." The motion detector under camera #22 continues its flashing. Checking the screen again, she is still unable to pinpoint the source of the problem. Alone and nervous, Wanda tries to talk herself through it. "Somethin' wrong here . . . maybe I ought to go down and look." Hoping whatever it is will just go away, Wanda pushes her chair back, tightens the belt around her small waist, unhooks the key to the bedroom, and makes a final sweep with the camera. "I waited a little minute to see if I was going to see anything." To Wanda's relief, the motion detector stops its warning signal in the bedroom, but before she can exhale in gratitude, another detector flashes on in the adjoining room. "It came on in the dining room. I was thinkin', *Oh Lord, something wrong here.* So I brought the camera direct to that table—still didn't see nothin'." The pitch of Wanda's voice rises as she remembers her attempts to catch the invisible intruder.

John praises Wanda's next move. "She's brave. She gets her flashlight, goes down the hallway, unlocks the door [to the Governor's Mansion display], and turns the lights on."

Wanda's cautious search reveals no evidence of the mysterious trespasser. "I looked all up under the bed; I looked behind the curtains." As she is about to leave, Wanda notices something peculiar. "I looked over towards the bed. The covers looked a little cranky." ("Cranky" is Wanda's wonderfully descriptive colloquialism for something messy or out of place.) Racing through Wanda's mind is the panicky notion that *Oh Lord, somebody or something's been here.* Backtracking, Wanda locks the doors and hurries back to the main security station to "start over from scratch."

Seated in the relative safety of her office, Wanda takes a few moments to reassess what's happened. The motion detector has stopped blinking, and she considers that maybe it has all just been a fluke; maybe the cleanup crew accidentally bumped into the bed and neglected to straighten the covers. But Wanda's comfort zone is rocked when the ghostly hijinks hit auto rewind. Now the motion detector under camera #21 kicks on. Wanda flips the video from camera #21 onto the big screen— nothing out of the ordinary appears. Then like a string of Christmas twinkle lights, the motion detectors in the hallway are set off in eerie progression, as if someone or *something* is passing by. Wanda is fearful. *Oooh, whatever it is, it's coming this way.* Staring intently at the camera monitors, Wanda fervently prays for a logical explanation for the bizarre phenomenon.

Nothing. Wanda knows she should be seeing something, any-thing, to explain the rippling lights on the motion detector panel.

The triggering of the motion detectors comes to an abrupt halt, indicating "it" has paused at the bottom of the great cast-iron staircase in the rotunda. "By the time the lights stop again at the stairs, I stick my head out and peep." Rhetorically Wanda questions, *Now, I'm assuming that it went upstairs, right?*

Wanda's worst fears are confirmed when she looks over her shoulder at the security board. The motion detector light under camera #30 flashes red, announcing that there is activity in the Senate Chamber on the second floor.

As the sole guard on duty, Wanda knows she must follow through. Carefully she winds her way up the imposing stair-case. At the top of the great rotunda, facing the front of the building, is the hallowed Senate Chamber. Garbed in her security uniform of dark brown trousers and white shirt, the solitary figure of Wanda Lee Porter approaches the massive oak doors. Wanda hesitantly places her hand on the silver door handle embossed with the state seal. She squeezes the lever, yanking the door open. Plunging in, she reaches over and quickly flips on the lights. The peaked roof and elaborate cypress millwork are illuminated by replicas of 1880s restorer William Freret's original gas chandeliers. The only furniture in the cavernous room is a small desk surrounded by a wooden guardrail, hug-ging the far right-hand corner. Over the desk hangs a portrait of a former senator, the Honorable Pierre Couvillon.

It takes a few seconds for Wanda to process the evidence before her. The chamber has been recently occupied. A dusty trail mars the gleaming surface of the polished floor. "I see these footprints as if somebody had walked from across the room towards the desk." Wanda's sole thought is, *Oh my God, they got a ghost in here.* Shaken, she rushes out, spiraling down the staircase, and grabs for the nearest phone. Wanda calls another guard to let him know "something is very wrong." Her second call is to Director Mary Louise Prudhomme to inform her that "something is in this building, and I don't know what it is . . . *whatever* it is, I'm going to get out of here!" Wanda's voice picks up pace as she catapults through the recital of events. Director Prudhomme asks Wanda to wait a minute, calm down, and stay there; she is on her way and wants Wanda to show her and explain what has happened. Wanda raises her eyebrows, questioning if any sane person would sit still in her position. Fortunately for Wanda, the backup security guard arrives for moral and physical support. The conversation between the two guards borders on comic relief given the evening's surreal content.

After listening to Wanda describe the blinking lights and the mysterious footprints, the backup guard asks her, "What do you think it is?"

Wanda bats the question right back. "What *you* think it is?" Both guards are skittish, as neither wants to be the first to acknowledge the presence of a ghost. Wanda sums up their brief stalemate. "I didn't want him to be thinkin' I was crazy, and he didn't want me to think he was thinkin' I was crazy."

Believing she has nothing more to lose when he asks a second time, Wanda blurts out: "A ghost, what else?" Shaking off goose bumps, she admits, "I never seen that like in my life." In a whispered aside she tacks on, "It really frightened me a whole lot. It really did!"

John Hoover winds up his story to the children by stating that security guard Porter must also write up a report on the incident, and the report is sent on to the secretary of state, Fox McKeithen. "A man, an alleged expert," says John with a small smirk, "is sent to check out the building. He goes up in the attic, spends about an hour and a half. He comes down and gives us a typewritten report that he has found evidence that *something* exists in the attic of the Senate."

John Hoover ends his tale to the visiting schoolchildren by telling them two things: "One thing I asked you to do when you first came in is not too make too much noise, because I never want you to wake Pierre during the daytime when I'm here, and second, I can't get Ms. Porter to work the night shift any-more." John says his tale usually works pretty well. The chil-dren are quiet for the remainder of the tour and he often spots them looking over their shoulders at the motion detectors. David Bonaventure, maintenance supervisor for the Old State Capitol Museum, is not amused by these stories, or by the antics of the ghostly Pierre. When the capitol building reopened its doors as a museum in 1994, there was a rush of tourists and researchers eager to check out the new Center for Political and Governmental History. Most visitors gazed in awe at the grand restoration honored by the American Institute of Architects. The impact of checkerboard black-and-white mar-ble floors, salmon-colored walls, and sage-green cast-iron fret-work, all crowned by the psychedelic swirl of a stained-glass dome in the rotunda, was mesmerizing. But David Bonaventure saw not what was in place but what was missing. "It was the crown," David points out. "It disappeared right after we opened."

The crown David refers to is not an adornment for the head of a king or queen, but rather a wide circular gold rim, part of the restored lights outside the Senate Chamber on the second floor. Two factors made this disappearance stand out: one, the missing "crown" was a rather mundane architectural element, not intrinsically valuable, and two, in order for a thief to have absconded with the gold banding, he would have needed a lad-der to reach it—or have the ability to levitate some twenty feet above the floor. Director Prudhomme says David prefaced his report to her about the missing gold crown with "I know you're going to think I'm crazy but . . ." Director Prudhomme states unequivocally that David Bonaventure is "a very practical guy, not given to jumping to supernatural conclusions."

For David, the most unsettling part about the string of miss-ing objects was not their disappearance, but rather their reap-pearance. Six months after the gold rim vanished, it reappeared in its appointed place gracing the top of the light. Leaning his five-foot-ten, tightly toned frame against the cinder-gray walls in the bowels of the building's basement, this maintenance specialist would also love to get his hands on Pierre's hidden cache of misappropriated tools. Perhaps he is just tidying up, but the persnickety Pierre has a proclivity for pliers. By last count David Bonaventure has "lost" fifteen pairs. "I'll put them down and when I turn around they're gone." Keeping up with the sticky-fingered Pierre's endless pranks is a full-time job, and David would just as soon send out for the nearest ghost buster. On Pierre's last foray into the supervisor's domain, David finally had a witness to the kleptomaniac tendencies of the capitol ghost.

A benefit was planned in the Senate Chamber for the Woman's Hospital of Baton Rouge. A key component of the decorations was an expensive painting arriving in its own custom crate. Maintenance worker Chris Beard lent a helping hand. Together Chris and David unloaded the crate. "It had instructions on top of the crate on how to open it and get the painting out. Chris and I read the instructions. It had a series of screws you first had to remove from the top; they were circled in black ink, like marks-a-lot. We got a drill and removed every one of those top screws, put all the screws on the table behind us, took the top off, removed the portrait from the crate, sat the painting against the wall, put the top back on the crate, grabbed the screws, and started screwing them back in." With a slight hesitation in his voice David adds, "we only had half of them. The rest of the screws were gone." David quickly rattles off the facts: "No one entered the room. It was just me and Chris. We looked for them everywhere for about five minutes—couldn't find them."

Not one to dwell on mysteries, David and his fellow worker went next door to his office, sat down to hash out a few more logistics for the evening's event, then returned to the storage room to get the painting. The first thing David and Chris noticed when they opened the locked door to the storage room were the missing screws lined up, like a regiment of soldiers ready for inspection. "They were laying on top of the table," states Bonaventure. "I have no idea what happened. All I know is that the screws showed up. Nobody could get in the room while we were in there or while we were gone." When asked for his opinion on supernatural phenomena, David scrunches up his pale face, the tips of his short mustache brushing his cheeks, and allows that "I went from a firm believer in not believing to—I'll believe just about anything now."

The down-to-earth Bonaventure is embarrassed over the notoriety such episodes have generated. His struggle to keep up with the packrat habits of Pierre was featured in a 1997 Baton Rouge newspaper article. During an interview for *The Haunting of Louisiana* television documentary, the camera-shy, thirty-something maintenance supervisor appears resigned to the constant ribbing by his friends over his scuffles with the capitol ghost.

On the other hand, Director Prudhomme has embraced the idea of a haunted building. The new marketing brochure features the capitol building basking under a purple night sky. An illuminated ruby-red glass window over the fortresslike front door beckons all those who dare to enter. The flip side of the brochure lists pertinent information about the museum, its exhibits and events, and in bold red, all caps, a single-line reminder: "DON'T FORGET ABOUT PIERRE—OUR GHOST." Prudhomme's rationale for placing Pierre prominently on the museum's brochure is: "People are interested in something beyond what's here today. They want to believe there *is* something for us to look forward to; certainly I think all of us do. So because of that, I believe it's a good marketing tool, and it happens to reach a lot of people."

At the same time, Prudhomme concedes not everyone agrees that hyping a ghost is good for the image. "We have had some negative reaction from certain organizations that do not feel that it is appropriate for us as a museum, or a center for political history, or a state facility, to be, quote unquote, 'advertising that perhaps there could be a ghost in the old state capitol.'"

Says Mary Louis Prudhomme with a pragmatic shrug of her narrow shoulders, "That's something you deal with, with almost everything you do. . . . It's had mixed reviews."

Shoring up her decision to promote Pierre, Director Prudhomme balances the negative with the positive: "Pierre [the ghost] has taken on a life of his own. He certainly was a respected person during his lifetime, so we respect him here. We try to be good to everybody—just in case. Right?"

10

Ile Phantom

Deep inside the murky labyrinth of Louisiana's coastal wetlands, swamp creatures of mythical proportions populate both Native American and Cajun lore. *"The loup garou, the feu follet, the coquin l'eau, the will-o'-the-wisp* . . . all the monsters live on that island right there."* As he skillfully guides his flatboat through overgrown logging canals, veteran captain Jerome Dupré points to their favorite haunt.

Ile Phantom, Ghost Island, is a minuscule spit of land floating among the marsh grasses of Bayou Segnette. Curtains of dusky Spanish moss dangle from haggard branches. Overhead a great blue heron circles the island, watching for movement below. Slithering through a mangled web of knobby cypress knees, a seven-foot gator slips into the tepid water. Palmetto thickets dotting the shoreline offer impenetrable hideaways for deadly water moccasins. Owls, turtles, nutria, raccoons, snowy egrets, ibis, wood ducks—all are mindful of the dangers within, and without. The wildlife of *Ile Phantom* is on alert for the traps and nets of marauding mortals seeking tidbits for their succulent gumbos. They pay little heed, however, to the ragtag band of ghosts and monsters, who seem intent on keeping humans off their island.

Dressed in baggy denim coveralls, a battered straw hat, and white fisherman's boots, Jerome Dupré is happiest trekking through the swamps on a quest for slumbering alligators. The man with the graying ponytail traces his lineage back to the original settlers of Acadiana. *Les Acadiens* arrived in the Bayou Lafourche area in 1785; they came from France, via a little side trip to Nova Scotia in Canada. These ancestors, along with their Native American neighbors, passed on tales of the legendary creatures who live on *Ile Phantom*.

On a "scary" scale the captain rates the *loup garou*, the Cajun werewolf, as especially dangerous. Dupré's lyrical Cajun accent flows like a looping roller coaster, each word hooking a ride with one that came before. When spoken by Dupré, *loup garou* eases into the more melodious-sounding *rougarou*. He also favors tongue-in-cheek Cajun-French logic: *je pensee, les ton passé les ton passé, quoique, que'qu'chose rester les meme* (I think, the time passes even though some things stay the same).

When dealing with the devilish loup garou Dupré urges caution, for the Cajun werewolf is capable of changing himself into any form at will. As a small child, the captain remembers being warned by his parents: "If you gonna go to Grandma's house, now you stay on that path. Now don't you step off that path because if you go out there to pick yourself a pretty flower, it can be a *rougarou*. And the *rougarou* is gonna change himself. He's gonna bite you on the neck, and you're gonna spend the rest of your life dancing with the other werewolves on Bayou Goula."

Captain Dupré tried the same warning on his own children, hoping, like his parents, to instill a little healthy fear of the real dangers inherent in the bayou. But the younger generation, says Dupré, think they are immune and far too sophisticated to believe in supernatural monsters. What they fail to understand, feels Dupré, is that stories of creatures who change forms and attack humans have been around for a long time and are shared by many cultures. The *loup garou* is a werewolf with a Cajun twist; he hangs out in the swamp, hairy arms oozing with mud. Rising on his hind legs, he bares his considerable fangs, seeking the warm blood of his next victim.

Another denizen of the brackish marsh is one Captain Dupré dubs the *coquin l'eau.* "It's a water devil. I can't recall anybody ever seeing a *coquin l'eau,* but *coquin* is like a devil—it's a type of devil in French—and *l'eau* is the water. So he lives in that water," and, warns the captain, "he'll do sneaky things to you. You might have yourself a real good meal, a fine repast and drink a glass of wine, or two or three bottles, and if you walk outside the house, he's the thing that trips you over, pushes you off the walk, makes you fall in the bayou. That's *coquin l'eau* that do that," nods the captain. "I understand," he says with a straight face, "that they're extending their range throughout the world." Dupré allows that *coquins l'eau* can have their pluses as far as monsters go. "It's nice to have them around. One night my buddy and I, we protected our family all night long. We couldn't hit them with full beer cans, but we could hit the *coquins l'eau* with empty beer cans. So we worked on that pretty good." Dupré spins yarns at dizzying speeds, from terrifying look-over-your-shoulder tales to I'm-pulling-your-leg-see-if-you-can-keep-up whoppers. The truth darts somewhere just below the surface.

Superstition cuts hefty inroads into Cajun beliefs and practices. Parents of young children are told to be particularly wary of the *feu follet* and to keep a stash of mustard seeds on hand to hold him at bay. Sitting in a cane rocker in his cabin near the bayou, twin baby alligators tucked under each arm, Captain Dupré shares his knowledge of the terrible *feu follet.* As Dupré weaves this supernatural tale, he works his own magic on the baby alligators; short, gentle strokes under the chin induce a somnolent state in the small creatures with the large teeth, a state in which they remain until the tale is over.

"The *feu follet* is supposed to be a child's spirit, a child still suckling from its mother when it died. It's an uncomfortable spirit. The *feu follet* is restless. What happens is that the Cajuns used to think that if their children would wake up with rosy [cheeks], that the *feu follet* had gotten into the room and was suckling on the children's breath." Captain Dupré continues to rock and stroke. The alligators' eyes are at half-mast and their closed mouths form smirky grimaces, wrapping from one side of their elongated snouts to the other; the effect is chilling. The fluid voice of the captain pulls the listener into a similar trance, as he explains how Cajun parents try to protect their children from this supernatural fiend who would suck the life's breath from their babies. To foil the evil *feu follet,* a traditional method of preventive medicine was carefully laid out. "What they did was scatter mustard seeds all around and underneath the bed. Before the *feu follet* could get to the children, it had to count all the mustard seeds."

The name of the inventive parent who first struck this bargain has been lost to the annals of folklore, but according to Dupré, forcing the child-snatching *feu follet* to count the mustard seeds saved many an innocent infant. "Mustard seeds are so tiny, like a speck of black pepper. And even if the *feu follet* got close to gitting all the count, he'd lose count, and he'd have to start all over again. So he couldn't get to the children."

Dupré stops his hypnotic massage and the limp bodies of the alligators snap back to life. Leaning over, he places the twin terrors into a large wicker basket resting on the wide planks of the cabin floor. Queried as to how he knows so much about the *feu follet,* he instantly responds, "O my God, I heard it since I was old enough to know that there was a *feu follet. Feu follet* is exactly like a *will-o'-the-wisp;* it slips in and out so fast, you can hardly see it. *Feu follet,"* pronounces the captain, is "like a fire spirit moving in the sky."

This talented raconteur launches into a personal narrative about the *feu follet.* "I remember this old black woman telling my mama . . ." The captain's story swerves now on a momentary detour. "We owned part of Delacroix Plantation down the Mississippi River. As a matter of fact, when we plowed the fields, we'd dig up spoons. They were so soft, they were made so pure of silver, you could wrap 'em up and curl 'em up like this." The captain demonstrates, taking an imaginary spoon and folding it into a ring around his finger. "Every now and then we'd dig up swords. Apparently there was some type of battle there, you know, a skirmish that took place, with all the horseshoes and the iron that we dug up. It was the original site of the antebellum plantation for the Delacroix family."

Dupré shoves a few wiry gray hairs off his face, getting back on track. "We had some enormous oak trees in the front of the house, possibly 300 years old. The old black lady, she told my mama, she said: *'Look one night; you're gonna see a light in those oak trees. You going to see a light coming through that tree up there and it's gonna be Mr. Delacroix, and he's gonna show you where the money is buried.'"*

Captain Dupré knows how to reel in his listeners with the best of them: a ghost *and* buried treasure—a captivating combination. "So one night, my dad wasn't there and here comes, we can see a light comin' through the trees. My mama put all the lights out in the house and made the children get underneath the beds. She was afraid, you know, that a spirit was out there. My mom was from Alabama; she wasn't familiar with all this voodoo stuff," though Dupré says his father's family had indoctrinated the children well. "We loved to be scared. They didn't have television until the midfifties so we would listen to the radio at night. We'd be listening to *The Inner Sanctum, Sam Spade*—so family stories of the *rougarou*, the *feu follet*, the *coquin l'eau*—all of those went together."

Years later, says the captain, he asked his mother why she told the children to hide under the bed when she saw the *feu follet*. Her reply to her son was that "she was just teasing and it was the moon coming through the trees." Captain Dupré does not buy his mother's explanation. "It doesn't seem like such a tease to me, you know. She didn't get out from under the bed and turn on the light until my dad got home."

And what about those tales of buried treasure? Back aboard his boat cruising by *Ile Phantom*, the Cajun captain regales tourists on his "Chacahoula Swamp Tour" with the exploits of local hero/villain Jean Lafitte. "Ghost Island got its name because the pirate Jean Lafitte supposedly cut someone's throat and buried them on the island. Now, the legend goes that wherever Jean Lafitte buried treasure, he also buried a man with it. The thing is, it's best to stay on his good side, you know, if you wanted to live and not be buried." Dupré gives an insider's view of the nefarious pirate's double dealing. "He [Jean Lafitte] is thinking if he killed one of his men and buried him there along with the treasure, they'd protect that treasure." Dupré pulls the throttle back to a full stop; the bow of the boat nudges the bank of *Ile Phantom,* placing the tourists dangerously close to the pirate's former lair.

The periphery of the island is marked by the stark white trunks of dying cypress trees, barren arms outstretched, beseeching the heavens for mercy. Salt-water intrusion from the Gulf, and the nutria with its voracious appetite for vegetation, have combined in a two-pronged attack on the delicate ecosystem of Louisiana's wetlands. The sudden "caw, caw, cawing" of a swooping black hawk heightens the ominous atmosphere. Dupré returns to the topic of ghosts. "You know, they'd be pretty mean 'bout having to die for that treasure. They claim people going on *Ile Phantom,* stepping on this island, looking for treasure, have been run off by ghosts, and the ghosts are dressed in pirate-type attire, turn-of-the-century clothing. The ghosts are dripping with seaweed and they run the people off. The treasure hunters would leave quickly for fear of their life."

All in all this is a plausible scenario for why treasure has never been found on *Ile Phantom*—or elsewhere in these parts. Dupré indicates a wide channel leading away from the island. "Bayou Segnette right here was the main path that Jean Lafitte came from his warehouses, hidden in the bayous, into the city of New Orleans."

Dupré paints a less-than-appealing picture of the dashing folk hero. "Most of the money he made, and his biggest commodity, was slaves. He'd attack slave ships and get the slaves aboard and then sell them at cut-rate prices to New Orleans' Creoles. They loved him. He didn't pay taxes, so he gave them a great price on all his goods."

As to what happened to the legendary Jean Lafitte, the captain shrugs, lifting his shaggy eyebrows. "There are two different legends. One for sure is that when he was run out of Barataria Bay back here, he set up shop in Galveston, Texas, and there are some who claim to be his descendants still living there. Another legend has him going to Central America and that he died capturing prizes."

The least-likely version Captain Dupré repeats is that Lafitte "moved to Missouri incognito and spent the rest of his life writing his memoirs." Captain Dupré says he'd be the first person in line to read them—if they ever come on the market.

Given the good captain's fondness for spinning an entertaining yarn, it would seem easy to discount his allusions to ghosts and monsters on *Ile Phantom*. Yet Ghost Island, steeped in swamp sorcery, is a compelling sight. Visitors are accorded fair warning. The boggy ground of the island is deceiving. One false step and you'll be sucked into the bayou *and* into the deadly embrace of the Cajun werewolf, the *loup garou*.

11

The Haunted Blacksmith Shop

Much is written. Little is known. Laboring prodigiously through the quagmire of lore surrounding the charismatic pirate Jean Lafitte, historians are at loss. *"Un Grand Peut-être*—A Great Perhaps." J. Frank Dobie comes closest to characterizing this illusive folk hero. Seeking closure to the haggling over the pirate-turned-patriot, a frustrated Dobie concludes in a 1928 article for *The Yale Review,* "He must have been a puzzle to himself." The baffling riddle that is Lafitte, Dobbie suggests, has supernatural overtones. "His strange career, his fabled hoard, and his uneasy ghost will not let his name die."

In a state where fact and fantasy are accorded equal measure, Lafitte's name is plastered everywhere, from a small town on Bayou Barataria to a national historic park. Lafitte's Blacksmith Shop and Bar, a landmark watering hole at 941 Bourbon Street in the New Orleans French Quarter, has long been a favorite stop. Herbert Asbury's 1936 guidebook, *The French Quarter: An Informal History of New Orleans' Underworld,* extols the locale as "a tourist shrine."

Although spirits at this celebrated Bourbon Street bar are more likely to be found packaged in a bottle than wandering loose, true believers swear Jean Lafitte has never left. Leaning on a barstool, hanging from rafters, swashbuckling through the courtyard, the pirate has been frequently sighted in the smoky haze of the dimly lit rooms. Patrons are known to raise a silent toast to the "Creole Robin Hood." Given the obsession and the setting (and a few hefty drinks), it's easy to envision the smug pirate, flask in hand, returning the salute. Such sightings may not withstand a sobriety test, but this does little to dampen the pervasive appeal of Lafitte's Blacksmith Shop and Bar.

Ghost researcher, Englishman Tom Duran, is suspicious when it comes to tales of pirates and ghosts. "The thing about them is that these stories were often concocted by the pirates themselves. . . . They were trying to scare people away." The pirates, says Duran, needed to sneak their loot in and out of the city under cover of darkness. "The last thing they wanted to encounter was people out for an evening stroll." Duran feels that the blacksmith shop on Bourbon Street was one of several locations where Jean Lafitte temporarily hid stolen goods. "Now, he [Jean Lafitte] obviously had a token blacksmith hammering away on a few bits of metal at the front, who hadn't got a clue what he was up to, but as soon as you walked past, opened the curtain in the back, the place was lit up by a sea of silver and gold." Stories of ghosts lurking about the blacksmith shop are, in Duran's estimation, "extremely dubious, to say the least."

The origins of this haunted site are as much a puzzle as the pirate himself. Historian/author Stanley Clisby Arthur raises issues of both title and use of the establishment. He questions if there was ever a fire roaring in the forge of the "so-called Lafitte Smithy." Tracking the earliest records of transfer of ownership back to 1772, Arthur was unable to find a paper trail documenting a link between the Lafitte brothers and the cottage on Bourbon. Discounting the iron plaque on its exterior wall proclaiming the locale as "Lafitte's Blacksmith Shop," Arthur writes, "The place has had many owners, but at no time did the name Lafitte or any of his men connected with his profession appear in any transactions having to do with this odd appearing, but typical structure of old, old New Orleans." Lafitte aficionados dismiss such minor discrepancies.

The building itself is an anomaly. Plucked from the raging fires of 1788 and 1794, the corner Creole cottage is a rare survivor. Roulhac B. Toledano's *National Trust Guide to New Orleans* lists the blacksmith shop among New Orleans' cultural treasures, but it more aptly resembles Dorothy's Kansas home after a crash landing in Oz. Its hipped roof squats on bulging walls ballooning precariously over the banquette (sidewalk). Two shuttered dormer windows sag despondently. The plaster has fallen away, exposing timbers slashing through soft brick, an early construction technique (*briqueté entre poteaux,* circa 1730).

At odds with the wrought-iron-balconied facades of its neighbors, the alleged hangout of Lafitte draws its fair share of stares from first-time visitors unfamiliar with the swashbuckling pirate. Then, as now, the cottage was divided, more or less squarely, into four rooms, each having French doors leading to the patio or street—a convenient feature for a pirate on the run.

As the first governor of the Territory of Orleans (the present state of Louisiana), Virginia-born William Charles Cole Claiborne was often perplexed and angry at Creole society's eagerness to embrace the outlawed Lafitte. On November 24, 1813, Governor Claiborne posted a $500 bounty for the capture of the shrewd pirate. Scoffing at such feeble tactics, Lafitte retaliated with a counteroffer of a $1,500 award for Governor Claiborne's head!

The late newspaper columnist Charles ("Pie") Dufour states in his epic history of Louisiana, *Ten Flags in the Wind,* that there was not "a shred of evidence" supporting the story of Lafitte's bold response to Claiborne's bounty-hunting techniques. On the other hand, Claiborne's disgust with the local citizenry over their loyalty to the outlawed pirate is well documented: "The apathy of the good people of the State, in checking practices so opposed to morality, and to the Laws and interests of the United States, may impair the fair character which Louisiana maintains." And, comments the sardonic ghost of Monsieur Lafitte, lounging in his namesake bar, *Plus ça change, plus c'est la même chose* (the more things change, the more they remain the same).

A forty-plus-member group dubbing itself the "Lafitte Historical Society" is on a mission to bring Louisiana's pirate legacy back to life. Customers at Lafitte's Blacksmith Shop and Bar are a bit startled when Rene Laizer, the leader of this new organization, strolls in. Dressed in "authentic" pirate attire, Rene assumes the role of Jean Lafitte, followed by his friends conspicuously garbed as Lafitte's brother, Pierre, and pirate captain, Dominique You. The members of the Lafitte Historical Society don pirate attire complete with swords, hats, and boots, as often as possible, and relish taking part in historical reenactments or simply sauntering about.

What is it about Jean Lafitte that instills such loyalty, breathing life into the specter? Lafitte's deification as the "Creole Robin Hood" notwithstanding, his "transactions" consisted of taking from the rich and selling back to the rich (at a handsome profit). There were no poor in this equation. Lafitte dined with high-ranking officials and prominent citizens, all anxious to shake his hand and seal a deal. These cordial relations, however, did not extend to the ladies; the only time Lafitte was permitted to mix with their wives and daughters was at the Victory Ball following the triumphant Battle of New Orleans. Naturally, such a prohibition only fueled the gossip among the women about this "romantic" figure. Darkly handsome, the rakish pirate claimed to be born in Marseilles, France, Bordeaux, France, or Port-au-Prince, Haiti (take your pick), circa 1780-85. Archival records offer few clues. The only area of agreement is that Jean Lafitte and his elder brother, Pierre, showed up in New Orleans shortly after the Louisiana Purchase in 1803.

In his quaint book, *Old New Orleans: A History of the Vieux Carré, Its Ancient and Historical Buildings,* Stanley C. Arthur refers to Lafitte as "The Gentleman Rover" and attempts to clarify his origins. "The claim that the Lafittes were of mixed blood is demolished by the fact that in each case the notary, and they were most careful about this in those days, did not identify any of the Lafittes, nor Pierre's wife as a person of color." Arthur sternly warns, "A great deal of foolishness has been written about these smugglers, but probably a lot more will be foisted upon a receptive public."

The most widely used image of Lafitte depicts a defiant figure looking askance, sporting a wide-brimmed hat and dark hair hanging in wavy ripples to his ears. The "Terror of the Gulf" is shown with arched brows shadowing large eyes, a slight hook to his nose ending in a long silky mustache, and a determined jut to his prominent jaw. His double-breasted, brass-buttoned jacket displays anchor insignias on the wide lapels. Lafitte's arms are crossed over his chest; in his right hand he clutches a spyglass. There is no substantial proof that Lafitte ever posed for this caricature.

At the opposite end of the spectrum is an illustration used by Raymond J. Martinez and Jack D. L. Holmes for their book, *New Orleans Facts and Legends*. Here Lafitte appears as a rotund, clean-shaven little man, possessing a double chin; a topknot of tight curls adorns his head. While Martinez and Holmes are careful not to completely exonerate Lafitte, because he *was* the leader of a "band of banditti," and as "guilty as the pirates whose plunder he sold," their assessment includes a curious denial of culpability: "It is doubtful that Lafitte ever robbed a ship himself or that he ever committed murder personally." Martinez and Holmes' quandary over Lafitte is evident. "Although he won glory at the Battle of New Orleans, he seemed impelled to follow his natural bent to plunder, to steal, to lie and to cheat." The authors seem to feel that Lafitte did not live up to his potential. "With his high intellectual capacity, his cunning genius, and his personal magnetism, he could have risen to a place of eminence in the industrial or political world." Back at the Blacksmith Shop and Bar, Lafitte's spirit would likely find this commentary on his character highly amusing.

The ghost of Lafitte must also ponder the persistent need of mortals to romanticize history. Serious researchers and writers have attempted in numerous articles and books to demystify the pirate. John Churchill Chase states unequivocally in *New Orleans, Yesterday and Today,* "The fact is neither Lafitte nor his brother Pierre was in the battle lines at Chalmette. He and his brother are supposed to have been defending one of the swampy approaches to New Orleans."

In reality, it was Lafitte's contribution of men and supplies to supplement Gen. Andrew Jackson's ragged forces that earned him a presidential pardon. His sentence as a smuggler was nullified, but it did little to line his pockets. By order of his archenemy W. C. C. Claiborne, Lafitte saw his funds confiscated, his warehouse at Grand Terre looted, and his ships seized. Disgruntled, Lafitte, with his band of Baratarians in tow, set up shop on "Galvez-town" island off the coast of Texas.

In his eminent chronicle *Lafitte the Pirate,* Lyle Saxon writes: "The mass of legendary material is so great and so disguised as history . . . it is rather like trying to put together a jig-saw puzzle, a portrait of a man which has been cut into a thousand fragments." A few of those glittering fragments speak of secret stashes of golden doubloons hidden along the way, igniting endless speculation about buried treasure and a pirate's ghostly curse. Other disjointed puzzle pieces plucked from popular lore dangle over this "Master of Deception": Lafitte hooked up with Jim Bowie, inventor of the famous knife, forming a scheme for the illicit importation of slaves to circumvent the Customs House in New Orleans; Lafitte was involved with the plot to rescue Napoleon from exile on St. Helena; Lafitte was an undercover agent for Spain; Lafitte continued throughout his lifetime and beyond to make clandestine visits to the blacksmith shop on Bourbon Street.

Naturally, the legendary pirate's final resting place is also the topic of many a wondrous folktale.

In a prehistoric Indian burial ground on a small bluff overlooking Bayou Barataria in Lafitte, Louisiana, under a lopsided iron cross, lie the remains of Jean Lafitte. To his right is the coffin of his cousin, Napoleon Bonaparte, and to his left lies his uncle, naval hero John Paul Jones.

Doubters and naysayers, take a number.

A more plausible, albeit less appealing, gravesite is a remote location on the Yucatan Peninsula where Jean Lafitte allegedly succumbed to yellow fever in 1826.

With no official final port of call on the manifest, pirate ghosts like Jean Lafitte appear doomed to maraud for all eternity. To quench these specters' Herculean thirst, occasional pit stops at a certain Bourbon Street bar are luckily within reach.

12

Little Girl Lost

Like Alice in Wonderland, the spirit of a young girl is trapped in the looking glass at the Lafitte Guest House. Overlooking Lafitte's Blacksmith Shop and Bar, this intimate corner hotel stands in quiet contrast to its bawdy neighbor. At the bar couples laugh and drink. Next door on the second-floor landing, a little girl cries. Her name is Marie. In the 1850s, a petite five-year-old lived with her family in this richly appointed four-story home. Marie has never left.

Downstairs in the Victorian parlor, wearing all the trappings of a nineteenth-century English gentleman—top hat, cape, walking cane, pocket watch—Tom Duran spins a poignant rendition of "Little Girl Lost." Duran, a former curator at London's House of Detention Prison Museum who now makes a living conducting historic tours, has an affinity for apparitions. While leading his New Orleans Ghost Tour through the French Quarter, he weaves the sad tale of a confused child who cannot seem to find her way out. Caught in a time warp, the small female ghost repeatedly exits a bedroom, walks down the hall, and passes through a gilt-framed, five-foot mirror mounted at the far end of the second-floor landing.

In his clipped British accent, Tom Duran recounts what

117

happens after guests check in: "People walk up the stairs and turn towards the mirror. They see behind them the reflection of a little girl. She's normally crying and when she appears, she appears as real as you or I. Of course, what people do is turn around to have a look at this crying girl, but there's nothing there. They turn back and look at the mirror and there's nothing there either. She has simply disappeared. And that happens time and time again."

As proof, Duran whips out a photograph. The enlargement captures a pale form curling around a doorway. Duran says Marie has been caught on camera at least four times since 1960. He confirms that she is always seen leaving the same room. "In the photographs that I've taken on my tour, she's floating out of what is today room 22. Rooms 21 and 22 were the former children's rooms," explains Duran. "In earlier times the children slept to the front and the adults slept to the back."

Duran thinks the waiflike ghost he calls Marie may be the daughter of the original owners, Paul Joseph Gleises and his wife, Marie Odalie Ducayet. Paul Gleises was a local businessman. Marie Odalie was a daughter of the prominent Ducayet family; the Ducayets owned a grand plantation-style home on the banks of Bayou St. John, just outside New Orleans.

When Paul and Marie Gleises moved into their new home on then-fashionable Bourbon Street, it boasted a traditional double parlor and dining room on the first level and six bedrooms spread over the second and third floors. The large attached wing at the rear of the home had rooms for the slaves and servants, a kitchen, carriage house, stable, and coal house.

Based on research by the hotel's current hosts and managers, Andrew Crocchiolo and Edward Doré, there were six Gleises-Ducayet children, but only three survived to adulthood. Crocchiolo and Doré also discovered that shortly before the Civil War, Paul Gleises transferred the deed to the house to his wife. Perhaps anticipating the ravages of war that were soon to befall the South, the couple packed up the remaining children, moving first to Philadelphia, then settling in New York. Paul

Gleises died in 1898 at the age of seventy-eight. The widow
Marie lived to the age of ninety. Little is known of what happened to the children.

From 1866 to the late 1960s, the house survived an assortment of owners until it was rescued by Crocchiolo and Doré,
who transformed the once-elegant Gleises home into a charming
hotel.

Researcher Tom Duran still has a dilemma. "The problem
I'm having investigating this haunting is that I've traced back
on the family records, and I've discovered a strange fact about
this household. . . . There were five little girls who lived here.
They were all called Marie. They all died before their fifth
birthday." Duran says several of the girls probably died during
the yellow-fever epidemics that swept through the city in the
summer of 1853 and again in 1854. New Orleans' cemeteries
are dotted with the tear-stained tombs of infants and small children, who succumbed to a grim shopping list of life-threaten-
ing diseases—cholera, tuberculosis, pneumonia, even the
common cold.

Duran believes that the miniature apparition in the mirror is
one of the little Maries who never got to blow out the fifth candle on her birthday cake. But at the moment, he has more questions than answers: Is the tiny ghost one of Marie Ducayet
Gleises' daughters who died in infancy? Or is she one of the
other Maries who lived in the house in later years? What spell in
the mirror lures the small spirit and holds her captive? The
English ghost buster swears, "I'll get to the bottom of it one day!"

Hauntings induce peculiar reactions. Just as in Lewis
Carroll's magical tale of *Alice in Wonderland,* odd things happened to the young actress who was recreating the role of the
diminutive ghost during the filming of *The Haunting of
Louisiana.*

With her finely chiseled features, fawn complexion, dark
hair, and luminous eyes, a local five-year-old was perfectly cast
as the lost Creole child, Marie. The television documentary's
director of photography, Oak Lea, was looking forward to

working with the diminutive and lively Cedar GrayHawk-Perkins; Oak had served as one of the elders at Cedar's naming ceremony. As the daughter of Annette, a member of the Sault Ste. Marie band of Chippewa, and GrayHawk, a tribal member of the Houmas of Louisiana, young Cedar had already participated in numerous Native American ceremonial activities and loved being in front of the camera. Both of Cedar's parents were there for the taping of the ghost sequence at the Lafitte Guest House.

As the crew worked on lighting on the second floor, the young actress happily laughed and played in the parlor. When grip Heather Genter came downstairs to inform Cedar and her parents they were ready to start, the carefree child lost her smile. The scene called for the actress to slowly walk past the doorway of room 22 and approach the mirror. Director Lea was positioned on the steps over the second-floor landing near the haunted looking glass. When he cued Cedar to start walking, she refused to budge. Lea stopped tape and knelt before the distraught child; tears pooled in her brown eyes, dribbled down her cheeks, and fell in tiny spatters onto her pink nightgown. Each attempted take ended with the same disastrous results: Cedar would tentatively place one bare foot forward in the carpeted hallway, look at the mirror looming over her—and freeze. The normally animated child would not speak, but only stare at the mirror and cry.

The precarious situation was partially resolved by placing Cedar's parents at either end of the hall. Leaving the comforting arms of her father, eyes downcast to avoid the dreaded mirror, Cedar aimed for the outstretched arms of her mother, waiting just beyond the frame of the camera. As soon as the take was over and she was free of the mirror's spell, the frightened actress reemerged as a bubbling little girl.

Did Cedar see something in the mirror none of the adults present could discern? Raised by parents with traditional tribal beliefs, Cedar has been taught since birth that all life is sacred; death is part of the cycle of life. Annette says this is not the first time her young daughter has "seen" something others could not.

13

Battles, Balls, and Bats

The sweeping Greek-templed facade of the raised cottage at 1113 Chartres Street, New Orleans, does double duty as a shrine to the memories of Civil war hero Gen. P. G. T. Beauregard and prolific author Frances Parkinson Keyes. Gen. Pierre Gustave Toutant Beauregard lived here briefly before and after the Civil War. In 1866, behind these walls in the secluded courtyard, a weary soldier began the preparation of his memoirs. Enamored with stories of the handsome Confederate hero, novelist Keyes moved into the vacant home in 1944, restored it, and lived here until her death in 1971.

By day, the tranquil gardens of this former residential enclave create a soothing oasis amidst the more raucous elements of the Vieux Carré. By night, alleged paranormal disturbances, led by the troubled spirit of General Beauregard, transform the museum into a battlefield.

Beauregard-Keyes House Museum director Marion Chambon insists there are no warring ghosts at this stately residence. Chambon's repeated denials have little effect on the passing parade of haunted-tour operators, who daily regale their avid listeners with grisly details. Juxtaposing historic facts with spectral conjecture, the legion of storytellers draws on

Beauregard's tragic life. The slender line between fact and fiction dangles and dips as reports of a haggard man stumbling through the house slide into sightings of Beauregard's soul tormented by visions of his fallen comrades and his lost loves, Laure and Caroline. The tales read like chapters in a Gothic romance novel.

Pierre's first wife and childhood sweetheart, Marie Antoinette Laure Villeré, a dark Creole beauty, dies giving birth to their daughter Doucette. Pierre believes that no woman could ever replace his beloved Laure, but at forty, he discovers peace and contentment with the demure Marguerite Caroline Deslonde. Pierre and Caroline are married in a quiet ceremony in May of 1860. They immediately set up housekeeping in the sunny-yellow French Quarter house flanked by fragrant gardens.

Personally and professionally, Pierre's life reaches a satisfying pinnacle. Rejoicing in his newfound love with Caroline, Pierre celebrates a much-anticipated milestone in his military career. On November 8, 1860, Maj. P. G. T. Beauregard is appointed commander of the United States Military Academy at West Point.

Beauregard's orders come through in January of 1861. Packing for New York, he makes a wrenching decision to leave his new bride temporarily behind. This loving husband is concerned about the unsettling effect of the country's escalating inner turmoil on his wife's delicate health. The days of compromise are slipping away. Bitter discussions of states' rights and slavery are about to shatter any illusion of peaceful resolution. Pierre is determined to protect the frail Caroline from the potential hazards of an arduous journey to the North, and he fears that his tenure as commander in chief of West Point may be short-lived.

On January 26, 1861, Louisiana secedes from the Union. Five days after he arrives at the military academy, the orders of Louisiana's native son are revoked. The loyalty of French-Catholic Beauregard, resident of a state aligned with the

Confederacy, is in question. Relieved of his post, Beauregard returns to New Orleans—and the waiting Caroline.

Pierre and Caroline enjoy a blissful few weeks together; Pierre encourages Caroline's plans for parties and outings. But their pleasant interlude is interrupted by a summons to meet with Pres. Jeff Davis in Montgomery, Alabama, the capital of the new Confederacy. Gathering his wife in his arms, Pierre assures a tearful Caroline he won't be gone long. The promise returns to haunt him. Beauregard's absence lasts four torturous years. He is never to see Caroline alive again.

Embraced by the army of the Confederacy, Beauregard is quickly appointed to the rank of brigadier general. He wins the hearts of fellow Southern rebels with his order to fire the first shot against Union-held Fort Sumter. This opening salvo on April 12, 1861 launches the Civil War. Beauregard's victory at Manassas gives further impetus to the Southern cause, yet by the bloody Battle of Shiloh in 1862, where one man out of every four is killed, maimed, or captured, the besieged general is grim.

Beauregard survives a series of illnesses on the battlefield, but the devoted Caroline, in poor health, cannot hold on. In 1864 while fighting in Florida, Pierre is notified by telegraph of his wife's death. Shaken, he staggers forward with his duties. Caroline's funeral is held without him. In the Deslonde family plot in Edgard, Louisiana, Caroline's tomb bears the epitaph she herself is said to have written: The Country Comes Before Me. *The Era,* a newspaper with Union sympathies, chastises Beauregard for abandoning his wife in her time of need. The biased article lashes out at Pierre as a man who "does not hold his oaths in high estimation . . . we find him not only plotting for the destruction of his country, but deserting his invalid wife for years leaving her dependent on others."

In *Madame Castel's Lodger,* her novel about the life of the Confederate general, author Keyes writes that this vicious report, belittling his devotion to Caroline, causes Beauregard "untold suffering." It is a suffering felt throughout the South as their cause meets an ignominious demise. The Confederacy collapses. After the war, the valiant hero returns to New Orleans with no job, no money, no wife.

Plagued by nightmares, Beauregard finds it impossible to sleep in the house he shared so joyously with Caroline. Nightfall finds him tossing the rumpled sheets aside and sitting on the edge of the carved rosewood tester bed. The images are unbearable: dying soldiers, many of them children—premature adults at eleven, twelve, thirteen years old—and a dying wife, laid in her grave before her grieving husband can bestow one last kiss.

A shaft of moonlight floats over the mirrored duchesse, shining on a miniature oval portrait Beauregard has carried everywhere. Caroline stares back with soulful eyes, her left hand resting under her chin. Her gentle presence fills the bedroom they once shared. Is it his imagination or did the sleeves on her delicate frock move? Or maybe it's just the edge of the muslin curtains fluttering in the faint breeze from the open window? Beauregard rubs his red-rimmed eyes. The sleep-deprived soldier falls into a restless routine: pulling on his boots and grabbing his shirt, he stumbles down the back stairs and commences a clockwise pacing of the courtyard below. The silence of the broken fountain, whose trickling waterfall once lulled the newlyweds to sleep, is disheartening. Even the wilting pink petals on the azaleas evoke painful memories of his gentle Caroline. Beauregard's depression deepens.

Rumors intensify about the gallant Confederate general haunted by his own past; the general's nightmares take on a supernatural persona. Long after Beauregard's death at the age of seventy-five, it is whispered that within the house, phantom battles rage unabated: cannons roar, gunshots boom, sword meets sword in clanging clashes of steel, voices rise in plaintive cries. . . .

Museum director Chambon is adamant that allusions to ghostly battalions careening through the house in a reenactment of the Battle of Shiloh, or any battle for that matter, are "ridiculous." Composing her hands on her lap, Chambon sighs; then in a muted tone she reluctantly repeats one popular tale that has a resurrected regiment of bloody soldiers on horseback charging down the center hall. To this frustrated museum

director, all such ghostly accounts are foolishness. Banishing
the rumors one by one, Chambon also nixes any possibility that
Pierre Gustave Toutant Beauregard steps down from his portrait over the marble mantel and joins in the fray. "I think it's a
story that got circulated and blown out of shape." Chambon's
voice rises. "I've been here almost twenty-one years and I have
never seen it." Tales laced with blood and gore make Chambon
cringe. "I don't want to see it, and if I did, I'd be out of here!"

Ghostly *battles* are definitely out at the revered Beauregard-
Keyes House; ghost *balls*, however, are allowed a little more lat-
itude. Rendering a sad portrait of the forlorn general in the
pages of *Madame Castel's Lodger,* novelist Keyes has him poring
over letters he and Caroline wrote during the war: they make
plans for a grand party upon his victorious return; he will
appear resplendent in his full dress uniform and she will don
her wedding dress adorned with flounces of "pink roses substi-
tuted for the white ones"; together, General and Mrs.
Beauregard will greet their guests on the upper portico, then
proceed to the great ballroom on the right side of the house;
the orchestra will strike up the "Beauregard Manassas Quick
Step," composed in honor of his great triumph; Pierre and
Caroline will lead the dancing and all eyes will be upon the
handsome couple.

Fate intervenes. Caroline dies before her husband's return.
The Southern cause is lost. There is no celebration in defeat.
The much-anticipated Beauregard Victory Ball is not to be—or
is it? Denied their celebration in life, the determined spirits of
Pierre and Caroline seem intent on having their party. The
Beauregards' shared vision for a gay evening in the ballroom is
so strong that fragments of the glittering nonevent are pur-
ported to be repeatedly seen and heard in the house: the high
pitch of fiddles, the light tapping of feet, the murmur of lively
voices, the sharp ping of crystal toasting crystal, the scraping of
chair legs on hardwood floors—sounds of a party in progress.

Compared to horror stories of phantom battles, these
reminders of happier times, whether initiated by ghosts or not,

are welcomed by Marion Chambon. "There are stories that in April a mist comes up in the ballroom here. You hear furniture moving, and you can hear music." Marion Chambon's favorite parts of this haunted dance are the scents. "You smell magnolias, sweet olives . . . and they have their ball." If there has to be a haunted event at the Beauregard-Keyes House, Chambon enthusiastically endorses the Beauregards' beautiful ball. "It sounds interesting. I'd like to see that!"

With a tinge of regret, the director explains what happens to the party atmosphere as the morning sun blazes through the floor-to-ceiling casement windows. "The mist dies down, the scents evaporate, and you're back to the empty room again."

Previous museum director Alma Neal was also an advocate of balls over battles. During a 1988 television interview with producer Barbara Sillery, Mrs. Neal spoke of guests, staying in the rear slave quarters, awakened by music coming from the main house. One woman swore she saw a transparent man in a Confederate uniform waltzing past the window with a lady in a misty white gown. Mrs. Neal felt that the true-life love story of the general and his lady lent an air of mystery and romance to the charming Creole cottage on Chartres Street.

If dreamy visions of ballroom dancers waltzing by offer little excitement to avid ghost groupies, in the truth-is-indeed-stranger-than-fiction category, there's always the Giaconas and some real-life blood and gore. For years a debate waged among the citizenry of New Orleans: whether to pin a medal on this tight-knit Italian family or lock them up for desecrating a shrine to a Confederate hero.

On June 18, 1908, *The Daily Picayune* reveals the details of a gangland-style massacre at "the historic old building known as the Beauregard Mansion where the great Confederate General dwelt." A graphic account of "one of the most dramatic of a long list of Italian feuds in the city's history" shocks the community: "The gallery was flowing with blood, while two bodies lay still and stark, an old man stood with his rifle in hand, with his son beside him, and down in the yard, at the foot of the stairway leading from the gallery to the court was another body." A wounded fourth victim escapes.

The old man with the rifle is Pietro Giacona, a native of Palermo, Sicily. Upon arriving in the United States around 1893, Pietro Giacona began importing wine as well as manufacturing his own wine from raisins. His clients are mainly Italian compatriots. The lucrative business enables Pietro to bring over his wife and children and comfortably settle the extended Giacona family into the spacious upper rooms of the old Beauregard mansion. The cool basement space on the street level is converted into a wine cellar.

Like the general before them, the Giaconas add another notch to the history of the celebrated house. Here's where the saga of a vintage gunfight rises a cut above the ordinary— Southern hospitality gone awry as Papa Giacona serves up a fatal volley of "Payback du Jour" to members of the Sicilian Black Hand.

Minutes after the last curl of gun smoke rises in the evening sky, the police arrive. The elder Mr. Giacona's version of the events was funneled through an interpreter (the Italian immigrant spoke not a word of English): Four men—Ciro Cusimano, Giovanni Barraca, Nuzie Barraca, and Francisco Vattali—came to his house on the pretext of checking on a barrel of wine. He and his son Carrado were cooling off with a snack of watermelon on the hot summer evening. Their "guests" barged in and invited themselves to dinner. Pietro protested that all he had left was bread and eggs; Cusimano and company said that would do for starters. Pietro sent his son to the kitchen to whip something up. The visitors seated themselves at a long table on the back gallery. The conversation drifted from pleasantries about the wine to a one-sided discussion of the merits and methods of just compensation. Demands for cash were punctuated with broad hints that human life was "as little value as the life of a fly." The elder Giacona, well aware he had already ignored a written demand from the Black Hand for $2,000 in blackmail money, tried to placate the diabolical men. Saying he would check inside the house to see what he could put his hands on, Pietro excused himself briefly, returning not a moment too soon. As he stepped back onto the gallery, Pietro spotted Ciro Cusimano drawing a weapon on his son. Pietro Giacona just happened to be cradling a fully charged Winchester automatic rifle. Cusimano cocked his revolver and missed; Pietro's aim was deadly.

"Death Knell of the Bloody and Odious Black Hand," *The Daily Picayune* touted the killing of the extortionists:

> Like wildfire the news that three members of the notorious Black Hand had been murdered and one other dangerously wounded spread throughout the city yesterday morning. Three corpses in the Morgue and one desperately wounded prisoner in the Charity Hospital attested to it, while the good Italians of the city were jubilant and lauded the deadly work of Pietro Giacona to the skies. He had, single-handed and alone, killed the three men and wounded the fourth, and such a deed could not but strike terror into the hearts of the fiends who had made life a burden to the careful, law-abiding and successful Italian citizens of the city.

Not everyone was buying into the lone gunman theory, or Pietro Giacona's claim that he was defending his son and Cusimano drew first. Police, scouring through the crime scene, were hard pressed to match Pietro's story to the evidence. The old man's amazingly accurate aim and claim of getting off only four well-placed rounds with his rifle did not tally with the ten bullets lodged in the bodies of the three slain men and the eight bullets found embedded in the walls, floors, doors, and courtyard of the Beauregard mansion. One additional bullet was retrieved from a gaping hole in the seriously wounded Francisco Vattali. Vattali fled the scene, but was easily apprehended. Police, following the trail of blood to a shed at the corner of St. Philip and Royal streets, found Vattali holding "a dead chicken to his left breast" to "draw out the inflammation and stop the bleeding." As he was taken to the hospital, Vattali protested he had nothing to do with the shootout; he was an innocent bystander struck by a flying bullet while passing the house. Curiously, Pietro Giacona amended his story to match Vattali's. Denying any knowledge of the wounded man, Pietro now swore only *three* uninvited guests appeared at his home.

Carrado Giacona, Pietro's son, also altered his testimony. Attempting to account for the extra bullets, he confessed to taking the rifle from his father, reloading it, then emptying it into the dead men. This still left police with no explanation for how a bullet of a smaller caliber than the rifle found its way into the body of one of the dead men.

The distraught widow Rosa Cusimano lashed back, telling police, "Pietro Giacona is a brute! He killed my husband. My husband was an innocent man; he was killed for nothing. He was invited to a feast at the Giaconas'. Pietro Giacona pretended to be a good friend of my husband and would kiss him when they met."

Faced with a paper trail documenting a four-month-long extortion racket headed by Ciro Cusimano, police were left to ponder if the late-night supper at the old Beauregard mansion was an impromptu visit by Cusimano and friends to collect a little "protection money" or a cleverly orchestrated plot by Pietro Giacona to lure the gang to his house and eliminate the competition.

While the police debated their course of action, a motion was taken under advisement by the Italian Vigilance Committee to present the Giaconas with a medal of valor for ridding the community of the scourge of the Black Hand.

But the Black Hand did not go quietly into the night. A year later, September 9, 1909, the remaining mobsters assembled for a little retribution.

Heavy blankets of humid air cover the city. No judicious dabs of perfume or frenzied fluttering of ladies' fans can overcome the smell of rotting refuse rising up from the streets. The inhabitants of the old Quarter flee to their courtyards or galleries, hoping to catch any token breath of fresh air off the river just blocks away.

Suddenly the oppressive silence is broken by a rapid, staccato gun-

shots as a gang of thugs takes aim at the front portico of the Giacona home. The whack of bullets is followed by anguished wails.

The gunmen in the drive-by shooting are Giovanni ("Vani") Barraca, Tony ("Joe") Barraca, Jack Veruso, and Joe Carbone, all relatives of the three men (Ciro Cusimano, Giovanni Barraca, and Nuzie Barraca) murdered by Pietro Giacona in the June 1908 massacre at the same locale.

In a scene straight from the Keystone Kops or even the Three Stooges, would-be assassins Vani, Tony, Jack, and Joe mistake abandoned chairs, draped in shawls on the upper front portico of the Giacona home, for people. The bumbling hit men take their potshots at phantoms. Their getaway vehicle is a horse-drawn "covered wagon" whose rear wheel falls off just as the police are arriving. Forced to make their escape by foot, they flee in scattered directions leaving a veritable sign-post of clues. In the rear of the wagon, police find a shotgun and empty shells. Faded letters on the side of the wagon lead the police to the St. Claude Avenue house of one Salvador Carbone. Salvador is not at home, but police take Mrs. Carbone and her eleven-year-old daughter, Josephine, into custody as material witnesses.

At the Jackson Avenue police headquarters, Josephine, who is described by the police as a "bright child" and "delightfully frank," identifies both the covered wagon and the horse with a white star on its forehead as belonging to her father. Chatting away, the youngster also tells police that four men, two of whom are named Joe and Vani, spent the previous evening at their house. Reluctantly Mrs. Carbone corroborates her child's story. Joe Carbone is her brother-in-law.

Police find and arrest Joe and Salvador Carbone at Joe's house. Salvador swears he was an unwilling participant in the assassination attempt. He merely served the gunmen "a maca-roni dinner" and sold them the horse and getaway vehicle. He became suspicious only when the four men shouted, as they were driving away in the wagon, that if they were successful they "would make a feast that night out of the Giaconas."

The police pay a visit to the widow Cusimano. Rosa now lives with her brother-in-law, Jack Veruso, one of the suspected gunmen. According to *The Times-Democrat*, when interrogated by the police, she states, "You police have done nothing to Pietro Giacona. He is out now; that is not just."

Poor Rosa. First the police and now her brother-in-law have failed to exact revenge for her husband's murder. Screaming, "God will take care of him yet!" Rosa Cusimano is led away.

Today guides conducting haunted tours past 1113 Chartres Street may have their facts a little skewed, but their allusions to gory massacres *are* on target. The alleged phantom screams and gunshot blasts heard within shouldn't be blamed on the nightmares of the beleaguered Beauregard; the more likely source is the spirits of the thwarted Mafia mobsters, condemned for all eternity to repeat their bungling attempts at retaliation. As for the Giaconas, their spirits hover in the courtyard rejoicing over a bottle of vintage wine. For they were the victors—on a sweltering June evening in 1908, during a singular repast, they eradicated the ringleaders of the notorious Black Hand, leaving the rest of their gang clueless.

Two tamer souls who prowl the property also feel they have earned the right to hang around. These four-legged phantoms with a proprietary air are canine and feline. Pointedly avoiding confrontation, they appear separately in various rooms of the house. The canine is Lucky and the feline, after some initial confusion, is known as Caroline.

Lucky, an adorable cocker spaniel, was the faithful companion of novelist Frances Parkinson Keyes. In the 1940s, Keyes, together with a group of civic-minded women, formed a foundation to restore the derelict temporary home of the revered Confederate hero, P. G. T. Beauregard. Cradling a copy of Keyes' *Madame Castel's Lodger*, Director Chambon muses that living in this house must have been "a writer's dream." Enumerating the advantages of a structure that has borne witness to a dramatic catalog of events, Chambon reiterates her affection for Beauregard—"a very romantic character."

Frances Parkinson Keyes stated in her author's notes that a poignant rendering of Beauregard was her "ultimate objective" as a writer. For eighteen years, she toiled over the Beauregard manuscript, determined to track down every lead. The aptly named "Lucky dog" followed Keyes everywhere—even through death's door. Keyes died in 1971 in the house, with the loyal Lucky guarding the foot of her bed.

Today the floppy-eared ghost still sniffs around seeking his mistress. Former director Neal spoke of staff members periodically complaining of a mildly offensive "doggy" aroma despite a strict no-dogs-allowed policy in the museum. No one yet has figured out how to enforce a ban on the ghost of plucky Lucky.

The museum prohibition on four-legged critters, be they real or imaginary, was also circumvented by a singular cat. Appearing one day in the lush walled gardens, the tabby sniffed the azaleas and settled in. Charmed by his gallant demeanor, the staff dubbed him "Beauregard," a name the tabby ignored. Underscoring his disdain for the designation, "Beauregard" gave birth to six kittens. With proof of their error dumped unceremoniously before them, they immediately renamed "Beauregard" as "Caroline" and allowed her to stay. The original "Caroline the Cat" eventually died, but in her memory a "Caroline" kitten is always given free rein to roam through the gardens, but never the main house.

Marion Chambon isn't sure if the feline ghost of "Mama Caroline" pops in to check on her descendants, but it's easy to tell when she's snuck back in the house. "We do have a little ghost cat that appears now and then, and she has a little bell on her." Chambon backtracks slightly. "I don't actually see her, I feel her, especially one time when she rubbed against my leg and made my dress move." By way of further explanation, Chambon says she was wearing a period dress and watched the bottom edge of the long full skirt move inward, as if a small body was pressing against it.

Chambon was in the middle of leading a tour and the group became increasingly curious when she kept looking down at her feet, attempting to shoo an invisible *something* away. Then, audible to everyone, came the tinkling sound of a small bell. To make sure there was no rational explanation, Chambon left the group, now peering under tables and chairs for the elusive cat, and went to the office to report that the current Caroline kitten had somehow gotten into the main house. The attendant on duty responded by saying that was impossible. The official kitten "Caroline" was contentedly napping under her desk.

Knowing that even nimble cats can't be in two places at once, Chambon returned to the tour group—and the playful four-legged spirit. "If I have to deal with a ghost," declares the accommodating museum director, "I'm glad it's a cat. I'm fond of cats."

Marion Chambon is not so accommodating when it comes to tall tales, especially the whoppers perpetuated about her neighbors across the street. The Old Ursuline convent is the only remaining French colonial building in New Orleans and, according to the *1999 National Trust Guide,* "the earliest in the Mississippi Valley." This 1745 complex with its rich history and sacred status as chapel and nunnery should merit some degree of immunity from fanciful lore. Maybe in historic Williamsburg or Philadelphia, but in *La Belle Dame Créole,* haunted tales are as convoluted as the dipsy-doodle curves of the Mississippi. After all, in the Crescent City the sun rises over the west bank and sets, in total disregard of conventional standards, behind the east.

As Marion Chambon looks over the gallery of the Beauregard-Keyes House towards the Ursuline convent, a heat-dazed gaggle of tourists labors to hear the dubious soliloquy of their flamboyant guide. Eavesdropping, this New Orleans native is appalled. "They say some ridiculous things . . . that the nuns are buried in the attic, in the coffins in the attic. At night they become bats!"

"I see nothing wrong with haunted history tours or ghost tours, and when combined with good theater or storytelling, they can make exceptional presentations that reflect an area's folk culture," states Maida Owens, the folk-life director for the state of Louisiana. However, she makes a distinction between folklore and "fakelore." "Folktales," says Owens, are the "traditions that have been passed down within a community over time," while "fakelore" is obvious commercial embellishment of the past. As the guardian of the state's rich storytelling tradition, she feels that "fakelore" shouldn't be foisted on a gullible public without some type of fair warning. "This is more about truth in advertising than anything else. I would simply prefer that the fiction be presented as fiction, instead of local tradition."

Marion Chambon remembers that when she was a child growing up near City Park, there was one traditional local tale about a house that always frightened her. "My mother would walk my two brothers and I through the Quarter and we'd stop at *The* Haunted House." Marion's mother would pass on stories about the angry ghosts of tortured slaves who haunted the building on the corner of Rue Royal and Governor Nichols.

To a little girl named Marion, *this* was where the ghosts truly hung out in the Vieux Carré.

14

The Haunted House

Thousands of winged creatures hover over the rooftops of the old Quarter of New Orleans; fluttering at windowpanes, they struggle to gain entrance. Their minuscule bodies and grasping legs lay siege to the onlookers below, coating faces, clothes, and exposed skin in a torrent of fear. A middle-aged couple from Michigan swats them from their eyes and ears, an intent older woman plucks them from her thick brows, and a young man holds his tattooed arm, with a Jesus Saves banner over a dripping dagger, aloft to ward off the airborne attackers. The ghost groupies have arrived at the high point of Tom Duran's haunted tour and are caught in a storm of swarming termites descending on *The* Haunted House.

The streetlight on the corner of Royal and Governor Nichols Street is a powerful magnet. Duran, the magician, takes full advantage of the spotlight. Flinging open his black cape, he pulls his group closer, using the wingspan of his garment to block the invading army of termites. "This," he begins in a stage whisper, "is the home of the evil Madame Delphine Lalaurie, heralded throughout New Orleans for her brilliant social gatherings." Here, the Englishman with the slicked-back hair pauses, making sure all eyes are locked on him. "It's 1832;

a neighbor is walking along, just about where we are standing." Duran points his cane to an arched transom over the carriage-way entrance. "Up above this door she spots on one of the staircases a woman she believes is Madame Lalaurie brandishing a whip. She's holding a seven-year-old girl and she's thrashing the life out of the poor thing."

The group momentarily halts its ensemble bug-swatting ballet to hear what happens next. "The neighbor is about to run and get the police, but the girl breaks free. Madame Lalaurie chases her. On the roof of this building, the little girl is panting, covered in sweat. She can't take the punishment anymore and she jumps into the courtyard behind me!"

Dozens of eyes follow the swishing motion of Duran's cape, arcing from the third-floor roof to the paved courtyard below. They share a collective shiver from the vision of the poor child's horrible death and the termites now creeping inside their clothing and down their backs.

This scene is repeated several times an hour as competing tours arrive to enthrall the uninitiated with their renditions of the nightly events at *The* Haunted House. Torture, dismemberment, skeletal remains, caged and manacled slaves—carnage too gruesome, too lurid to be true—but, it is.

In nineteenth-century Creole New Orleans, appearances were paramount. Gilded invitations to court or be courted, to be wined and dined, or to attend exclusive tête-à-têtes were the epitome of social status. The thrice-married Madame Delphine Macarty de Lopez y Angula Blanque Lalaurie presided over many of these fashionable affairs.

In a city known for its laid-back tolerance, there were rumors that all was not as it seemed in the Lalaurie household. While Dr. Lalaurie's wife was brought up on charges and fined several times for the harsh treatment of her slaves, this was an example, Duran points out, "where the rich can get away with anything." *Almost* anything.

On April 10, 1834 a fire breaks out in the Lalaurie mansion and the true horror of Delphine Lalaurie's secret life is exposed; the lady of the house not only reveled in throwing parties, she also took perverse pleasure in the pain of others.

Volunteer firemen and police arrive and encounter cruel evidence of Madame Lalaurie's sadistic nature. One reliable eyewitness, a Judge Canongo, reaches the scene moments after the fire starts. Hearing there are slaves chained within who would perish in the conflagration, he immediately approaches the Lalauries and asks if this is true—are their slaves imprisoned in the garret? Rudely rebuffing the judge, Dr. Lalaurie declares it is all slander.

Later, in a sworn deposition, Judge Canongo testifies to the "atrocities" uncovered at the Lalaurie household. "Two negresses were found incarcerated . . . one of the negresses had an iron collar very large and heavy, and was chained with heavy irons by the feet . . . another old slave was found who had a deep wound on the head." Accounts differ on the exact death toll; some reports say seven bodies were found and the remaining slaves were so mangled and disfigured, they spent their final days in agony. The "appalling spectacle" of the tortured slaves takes a ghoulish turn. The Friday morning, April 11, 1834, edition of the *New Orleans Bee* notes: "Four thousand persons at least, it is computed, have already visited these victims to convince themselves of their sufferings."

Although local papers brand the infamous Delphine Lalaurie "a demon in the shape of a woman," Madame L. is not immediately arrested. Haunted-tour operator Tom Duran says that in deference to her social status, she is simply asked to "come down to the police station in a couple of days to give a statement."

New Orleans Bee publisher Jerome Bayon was having none of the kid-glove treatment. His April 11 editorial provoked public indignation to a frenzy. "Seven slaves more or less horribly mutilated, were seen suspended by the neck, with their limbs apparently stretched and torn from one extremity to the other. Language is powerless and inadequate to give a proper conception of the horror . . . we feel confident that the community share with us our indignation and that vengeance will fall, fall heavily upon the guilty culprit." Bayon has his wish the next day: "The populace have repaired to the house of this woman, and demolished and destroyed everything upon which they could lay their hands. At the time of writing this, the fury of the mob remained still unabated and threatens the total demolition of the entire edifice."

Dr. and Madame Lalaurie, who fled the house immediately after the fire, return, sneaking back through the courtyard entrance on Governor Nichols Street. They toss a few prized valuables in their carriage, throw open the gates, and thunder out, barreling through the outraged crowd. The mob vents its anger on the home. Stumbling over each other, they toss Madame's cherished possessions out of the windows to the streets below. Celebrated writer George Washington Cable offers vivid details in his collection *Strange True Stories of Louisiana:* "In a single hour everything moveable disappeared or perished . . . tables, chairs, pictures, pianos . . . were hurled out . . . and smashed into a thousand pieces." The uncontrolled throng was "in the act of pulling down the walls when the sheriff intervened . . . and put an end to their work."

The once-elegant Lalaurie townhouse is further desecrated with graffiti scrawled on its burnt walls. In Cable's 1888 account, he quaintly describes the insults as "writings of indignation and just punishment." Neighbors cross to the other side of the street rather than risk brushing against the building. Tales mount that the skeletal remains of twenty-five adults and one small child are buried beneath the flagstones of the inner courtyard. The haunted house has become a midnight rendezvous for their tormented souls: moans and clanking chains permeate the building, mangled phantoms pace the gallery, and—most heartbreaking of all—the ghost of a little girl races round and round the roof trying to escape the evil clutches of Madame Lalaurie.

What drove this woman, surrounded by life's luxuries, to such cruel atrocities? Was she truly evil incarnate or the much-maligned target of nineteenth-century tabloids? Historian S. C. Arthur comes to her defense: "The mistress of this home was the first victim of yellow journalism in this country . . . she was far from being the fiend tradition has labeled, or should we say, libeled her."

As a child, Delphine learned to bear up under a mantle heavily encrusted with proper names. She was born Marie Delphine Macarty to the well-respected Louis Barthélemy Chevalier de Macarty and Marie Jeanne Lovable Macarty, but little is known of her early years other than that she had four siblings. The records of St. Louis Cathedral confirm the young Delphine's first marriage to Don Ramon de Lopez y Angula on June 11, 1800. The groom is listed as a "Caballero de la Royal de Carlos," son of his Lordship Don José Antonio de Lopez y Angula and Dona Ana Fernande de Angula. Don Ramon and his bride, Delphine, were welcomed into the glittering social whirl of *La Nouvelle-Orléans*. In 1803 ownership of the Louisiana colony was transferred to the United States; Don Ramon, a native of Galicia, Spain, was appointed Spanish consul general to the new American territory and received a royal command in 1804 to take his place at the Spanish court. In a flurry of excitement, Don Ramon and Delphine booked passage to Madrid.

Two unscheduled events alter their course forever; neither Don Ramon nor Delphine ever make it to Spain. Don Ramon dies mysteriously as the ship pulls into Havana, Cuba. In Havana, a pregnant Delphine gives birth to her first child. The tiny baby is christened Marie Delphine Borja Lopez y Angula de Candelaria, bearing the names of her mother and her father's grandmother, Dona Francisca Borja Endecis. As soon as she is able to travel, the widow Delphine returns to New Orleans with her daughter, "Borquita"—"little Borja."

Four years later, in 1808, the widow Marie Delphine Macarty de Lopez y Angula marries her second husband, the wealthy Jean Blanque, who had arrived in New Orleans from France five years earlier. Delphine dutifully bears him three daughters and a son: Marie Louise Pauline, Louise Marie Laure, Marie Louise Jeanne, and Jean Pierre Paulin Blanque. Delphine's talented husband earns his living as a banker, lawyer, legislator, and merchant. The reported source for much of his "merchandise" is none other than the pirate Jean Lafitte. Jean Blanque provides his lovely wife with two lavish homes, a townhouse at 409 Royal Street and a country retreat downriver from New Orleans. The arrangement works well for eight years, until he abruptly dies in 1816.

The next we hear of the twice-widowed Marie Delphine Macarty de Lopez y Angula Blanque is in 1825 when she marries husband number three, a Dr. Leonard Louis Nicolas Lalaurie. Dr. Lalaurie, a native of Villeneuse-sur-Lot, France, operates a successful medical practice in New Orleans. Somewhere around 1832, Dr. and Mrs. Lalaurie move into 1140 Royal Street with her five children: "Borquita," from her first marriage, and the son and three daughters from her second. Delphine Lalaurie quickly establishes herself as the "Queen Diva" of parties; the elite jockey for invitations to her lavish affairs. There is some disparaging gossip and jealousy. Those who reside in the American sector frown on the snobbish ways of the French and Spanish of the old quarter, and there are hints that Madame Lalaurie has a peculiar fondness for inflicting pain. While presenting her party face to society, this woman with the Dr. Jekyll-and-Mr. Hyde personality excuses herself from the table to take another stab at a hapless slave.

The fire of 1834 threw back the curtain on the macabre backstage machinations of the insidious Madame L. Years later she is spotted dining in Paris. The most accepted theory holds that, after jumping in their carriage, Delphine Lalaurie and husband number three flee to the north shore of Lake Pontchartrain, board a schooner for Mobile Bay in Alabama, and from there catch a ship to France.

Back in New Orleans the citizenry are busy ransacking the home of this maniacal woman, but Delphine Lalaurie never forgets the place where she reigned at center stage. Her final request on December 7, 1842 is to be allowed back in. Marie Delphine Macarty de Lopez y Angula Blanque Lalaurie is not to be denied. Her body is secretly buried in St. Louis Cemetery No. 1, on the fringe of the French Quarter.

The Lalaurie mansion on Royal Street has endured a far less peaceful fate. Its haunted reputation is so imbedded in the very fabric of the house that not even well-intentioned renovations can erase the awful deeds committed within. The *National Trust Guide to New Orleans* states that, begun as an innocuous two-story residence for an Edmond Soniat DuFossat, the unfinished house was sold on August 30, 1831 to Madame Delphine Macarty de Lopez Blanque Lalaurie. Local lore says Barthélemy Chevalier de Macarty gave the home to his daughter Delphine on the occasion of her third marriage. If this is true, it must have been a very belated wedding present, as Delphine had married Nicolas Lalaurie six years earlier, in 1825. It is generally agreed, however, that Madame Lalaurie was definitely in a party mode at 1140 Royal Street from 1832 to 1834, and that the fire of 1834 revealed the work of a twisted mind.

Incredibly, during her flight from the angry mob, Delphine Lalaurie managed to stop long enough to sign a power of attorney, turning the property over to her son-in-law Placide Forstall, husband to her daughter Borquita. For the next three years, the ransacked building hung its head in shame—no one wanted to live in a house of horrors.

Between 1837 and 1866, three brave individuals attempted to make the house a home again. Pierre Edouard Trastour redesigned the burnt hull in 1837, adding a third floor and enhancing the facade with French Empire architectural elements. He sold it quickly to Charles Caffin. Like a hot potato, it was in turn passed on to the widow of a Horace Cammack in 1862.

Sometime after the Civil War, during the era of Reconstruction, the much-maligned home was selected for a noble, if not ironic, experiment in progressive education. Journalist George W. Cable claimed to have actually sat in on one of the mixed-race classes. "There in the rooms that had once resounded with the screams of Madame Lalaurie's little slave fleeing to her death . . . the daughters of two-widely divergent races" were sharing the "common enjoyment of public education." This early attempt at integration, pre-New Orleans Public School System, lasted until 1877 when the "separate-but-equal" notion of education was introduced.

The next movement to purge the evil from *The* Haunted House soared on a more harmonious note. Madame Lalaurie's dining room echoed once again with sweet music; in 1882 the home was revamped as a music conservatory. However, says Cable, the haunted spirits were still there, although dancing now to a gentler refrain.

In a state where ghosts have always had a curious impact on the economy, an Italian entrepreneur aptly named Fortunato Greco saw an opportunity and ran with it. Greco's operation of "The Haunted Saloon" at a downstairs corner of the Lalaurie mansion enjoyed moderate success lasting from 1893 to 1916. Greco's advertising campaign, in English and Italian, challenged customers to test their fears: *There is an end to everything, so there is with ghosts. Come and be convinced. Ten Cents.* It was not a bad marketing gimmick for its time.

A few ups and downs later, *The* Haunted House was again witness to hard times. During the Great Depression, philanthropist William J. Warrenton set up a refuge for indigent men inside the vacant rooms. The men were not always grateful for their accommodations; some apparently preferred sleeping in the street to having their slumber interrupted by restless spirits.

Currently the three-story townhouse presents a subdued demeanor. The 1976 and 1980 restorations were guided by the architectural firm of Koch and Wilson. Access is denied to the general public. The recessed front portal is guarded by a locked iron gate. The only concession to its ranking as *the* number-one haunted house in New Orleans, a must-see on every haunted tour, is a simple handwritten note posted over the doorbell: Private residence. Not open for tours. There is one grisly final footnote to this tale of horror. There have been reports of recent sightings of the sadistic ghost of Madame Lalaurie returning to her former home. Masking her identity behind a dark veil of Spanish lace, she slithers by, eavesdropping at shuttered windows for the tormented cries of her mutilated slaves.

15

The Ghostly Decorator

Not all of the New Orleans French Quarter's spirits are intent on evil. Surveying the Victorian elegance of the double parlor in the Lanaux Mansion, Ruth Bodenheimer is well pleased with the decorating flair of her ghostly housemate. "Mr. Charles Andrew Johnson built this glorious house in 1879. He was a wonderful gentleman and a practicing attorney. . . . There was not a Mrs. Johnson so he did all this decorating himself."

Ruth's generous compliment is not totally accurate, as she neglects to take a bow for her own considerable efforts. The ongoing restoration of this Renaissance-Revival townhouse on Esplanade Avenue at the edge of the French Quarter is an interesting collaboration combining some "spirited suggestions" from a fastidious ghost and lots of "implementation" from its mortal owner.

Insisting on giving full credit to the phantom Mr. Johnson, Ruth Bodenheimer reiterates, "It's always his guiding hand. I always say he is my partner in caring for the house, because he knows exactly what I'm doing." The novelty of having a personal decorator on call is surpassed only by the realization that these tasteful tidbits arrive via a spiritual hotline from the netherworld.

Despite their close-working relationship, Ruth Bodenheimer maintains a respectful formality with Mr. Johnson, never lapsing into the more casual mode of addressing her gentleman ghost as Charles or Charlie. Sitting down on the plum-colored settee, she explains how it works. "He's instrumental if I have a major project, especially if it's a costly one. I'll have little private chats with him."

Mr. Johnson's black-velvet top hat rests on a small marble-topped tea table, as if he has just stepped out of the room. Leaning over and giving the hat a friendly pat Ruth talks about her first successful consultation with her ghostly decorator. "I said to him, 'You know the finances and the funds. Do you think we can find a twenty-one-by-fourteen-foot rug for the dining room at a fair price?' That was my first experience and he did!"

Visions of magic carpets à la *Arabian Nights* floating through the door notwithstanding, the actual feat was accomplished minus the overt dramatics. The source for the perfect dining-room floor covering "came" to Ruth via a little subliminal message from Mr. Johnson. She immediately headed to the store and found precisely what she needed—a rug at a discounted price. Ruth laughs at the notion that it was merely a lucky coincidence. She and Mr. Johnson have been at this for quite some time.

Ruth tracks her love of Mr. Johnson's house back to the 1950s when she met then-owner Louella Wieland. Acting as a mentor for the young Ruth Bodenheimer, Ms. Wieland taught her protégée that a woman can do things on her own and in 1986 encouraged her to purchase a half-interest in the land-mark building.

Three years later, in 1989, Ruth was able to secure financing to buy the remaining half of the home, becoming the sole owner—or so she thought. Louella Wieland neglected to men-tion the haunting presence of a third party to their arrange-ment. Ruth's "new" housemate sedately went about his business—until she set about making the dust fly.

Louella Wieland had been meticulous in overseeing structural repairs to the exterior of the historic Esplanade townhouse, but decorating was not her forte; the interior of the 12,000-square-foot residence was a haphazard affair. "The whole time she lived here I don't believe she put curtains on the windows or rugs on the floor," says Ruth, describing Louella Wieland's bare-bones style.

A suite of three rooms on the second floor was first on Ruth's decorating agenda, for this was to be her private living quarters. As an executive at a local steamboat company, she was known for her organizational skills and quickly applied her talent for making the impossible a reality at her new home. However, the specter of Mr. Johnson was less confident in her capabilities and clearly felt that Ruth needed a guiding hand to ensure that his impeccable taste in interior design was followed to the letter. He left a lengthy paper trail as a ghostly template for her to follow.

As Ruth began rummaging in the attic she discovered a large number of books with curiously earmarked passages. "I was finding these books Mr. Johnson left behind. . . . I learned he had a passion for drapes, carpeting, upholstered furniture. . . ." Having previously worked at a large New Orleans auction house, Ruth was especially thrilled to realize she and Mr. J. shared a love of Victorian antiques. For her, the books were Mr. Johnson's means of communication, the method he utilized to point her in the right direction. "To sit at two o'clock in the morning and read a book he underscored, it told you exactly what he was thinking." Ruth reverently picks up an 1878 edition of *Modern Dwellings in Town and Country,* showing where Mr. Johnson marked sections on how to arrange the furniture in the rooms. All of her "reference books" bear the spidery signature of *Charles Andrew Johnson* or, if he was in a hurry, the initials *C. A. J.*

The well-to-do bachelor was also fond of travel, making numerous trips to London and Paris. Gently caressing another book, Ruth points to Johnson's notations in the margins commenting on his specific preferences in food, lodging, and architecture. He was a man, she believes, who spent a great deal of time observing details and now, to Ruth's intense delight, he keeps his keen eye focused on her. "I always talk freely in front of Mr. Johnson, because I feel at some point in time, if it's a question that I have, if it's something I want to know about the house, somewhere the answer is going to appear, whether I'm reading one of his books or just wandering through the rooms. His fingerprints are all over the house."

It is not unusual, says the dignified owner of the Lanaux Mansion, to find her at two o'clock in the morning sitting downstairs in the gold-draped parlor dominated by an ebonized nine-foot grand piano—waiting for a signal from Mr. Johnson. "I think I am carrying on the decorating of the house as close as it's ever been to 100 years ago," but, states Ruth Bodenheimer with no hesitation, "I think I would have liked his decorating better."

Ruth is committed to pleasing her ghostly decorator. In 1991, she hosted a party to commemorate his 172nd birthday. The celebration also marked the return of Mr. Johnson's portrait, which had been removed from the home in 1953, the year the Lanaux family moved away. The invitation to the birthday celebration read: *Welcome home Mr. Johnson. You have been absent thirty-eight years.*

The portrait also cleared up a mystery bothering Ruth. The one and only time this very practical woman had seen a physical manifestation of a ghost in the house, she wasn't positive who, or what, she was looking at. "It was a typical Saturday morning, and of course I was very busy working upstairs, and I came out of my bedroom and started down the hall to get something on the first floor." As Ruth reached the landing to the stairwell, something caught her attention. "It" was slowing ascending the staircase to the attic on the third floor. "I saw a vision, sort of a very misty vision. I wasn't frightened by it."

Three months later, Ruth got a call from a member of the Lanaux family, who heard she was restoring the home and told her his father, eighty-five-year-old Gaston Lanaux, had the original portrait of Charles A. Johnson. Ruth immediately went to see the portrait and came face to face with her ghostly manifestation on the stairs. "The vision I saw was of a man wearing a short jacket, like an English walking coat, cropped right above his knees. And when I saw Mr. Johnson's portrait that's what he had on." After promising to rehang the 1885 oil painting in its original position in the parlor, Ruth was able to "bring Mr. Johnson back home."

Thinking back on her ghostly vision on the stairs, Ruth Bodenheimer's face glows. "It was definitely Mr. Johnson. I think he was saying to me, 'I know how hard you work on this house and I know it's a pleasure of insanity. Good job.'" With a satisfied laugh, she adds, "I really think he was trying to tell me that."

The single sighting of her phantom housemate is a slight disappointment, but, surmises Ruth, he is probably just a little shy. "He was a very private man. He had no children." Consequently, Ruth believes, he poured all his love into, and continues to devote himself to, his home.

Yet there is still another unresolved mystery connected to Mr. Johnson's residence. To offset restoration and operating costs, Ruth Bodenheimer with her husband, Ken, opened the hundred-plus-year-old-home to bed and breakfast guests. They needed a name befitting this impressive heirloom of nineteenth-century New Orleans, and one that would lure visitors.

Poring over notarial records and Mr. Johnson's papers, Ruth discovered that the bachelor had bequeathed his home to a lovely young woman. Curious, Ruth delved a little further into her ghost's personal affairs. "In 1896 when Mr. Johnson was gravely ill, he invited Marie Andree Lanaux to move into his house to care for him." Ruth is quick to explain that all proprieties were observed. "At that particular time, Marie was married to George Lanaux and had one child. When Mr. Johnson passed away in the home, Marie inherited his entire estate, including the house. Marie had four additional children, and she lived here until her death."

If Ruth knows more about the link between the older Charles Andrew Johnson and the younger Marie Andree

Lanaux, she's not telling. However, in a 1994 interview for a local paper, Ruth did allude to a mysterious envelope listed among the possessions in Mr. Johnson's will. The contents of the envelope will never be known, as the instructions written in Charles Andrew Johnson's distinct script clearly stipulated, "The envelope is to be destroyed unopened upon my death." The house on Esplanade and Chartres is the only tangible proof of Johnson's devotion to Marie.

Ruth Bodenheimer christened the home the Lanaux Mansion because there were so many generations of Lanauxs who had grown up in the home and, she concedes, it has a more evocative ring than the more mundane-sounding "Johnson House."

In spite of this bit of fudging with names, Ruth remains steadfastly loyal to Mr. Johnson. Guests given a guided tour of the formal rooms on the first floor are always first presented to a gold-framed likeness of the distinguished gentleman seated in the parlor, coat precisely arranged and spectacles in hand. Ruth admits she speaks so often in the present tense of Mr. Johnson, many people believe he is a flesh and blood family member living in the home. She pokes fun at those who look at his portrait and claim they too can sense his presence, because they feel a warm spot in the room. Says a smiling Ruth, "The room is warm because I have the heat on."

Ruth holds out hope that Mr. Johnson will overcome his shyness and put in another personal appearance. "I would like to think that Mr. Johnson could walk through that door this evening and I would be so glad to see him. I wouldn't think that strange at all." In the meantime, she remains grateful to her ghostly housemate for his impeccable decorating tips.

Ruth Bodenheimer identifies so closely with Mr. Johnson's era that she inadvertently began her interview for the television documentary with "When *I* first moved here in *1896 . . .*" Ruth just shrugs at the Freudian slip teleporting her back a hundred years. "Some people might think I'm absolutely crazy," acknowledges the serene owner of the Lanaux Mansion, who firmly believes that "the past is part of us today."

16

The Singing Monk

Topping the charts on Louisiana's Haunted Hit Parade is New Orleans' own singing monk. His baroque baritone vocals have been hitting the ghostly high notes since 1776, making Père Dagobert de Longuory one of the oldest-known specters on the scene; this stellar performer holds his nightly open-air concerts in an alley next to St. Louis Cathedral.

He sings a cappella. Church bells, calliopes, ships' horns, brass bands, Mardi Gras mambos, and raucous crowds occasionally mask the heavenly sounds of this singular virtuoso. Those who patiently wait along the iron railing bordering St. Anthony's garden to the rear of the cathedral are often rewarded with an inspired rendition of the *Te Deum* or the *Kyrie eleison*.

The soft slap of sandals on the massive slate slabs lining the alley is the first hint the singing monk is on his way. Like a mist curling and creeping off the river, the specter slowly takes shape as the metamorphosis from fog to human form is complete. Clad in the coarse brown robe of the Capuchin monastic order of religious, he stands with his large hands joined in supplication. The breathless watch in awe as his tonsured head tilts back, his lips part, and, one by one, each glorious note rises from his throat linking melody, harmony, and rhythm in

angelic chords. But as with every true artist, Père Dagobert de Longuory has not always been appreciated or understood.

When the starry-eyed monk arrived in the French colony of Louisiana in 1743, the vast wilderness of the new territory was rife with the highly combustible commodities of politics and religion. Assigned to the Capuchin mission in Natchitoches, the young friar got his first dose of the opposing factions within the Catholic Church. The Jesuit missionaries fumed they should have an exclusive on converting the heathen and preaching to the settlers—they were after all the first on the scene. The Capuchins believed there were more than enough lost souls to be rescued, and refused to budge. This turf war between the Capuchin monks and the Jesuit missionary priests would undermine Père Dagobert's entire ecclesiastical career.

By 1744 the dedicated Fr. Dagobert de Longuory was elevated to the rank of superior of the Capuchin missions and appointed rector of the newly built Church of St. Louis in New Orleans. Either through naiveté, or an honest attempt to clarify spiritual jurisdiction, Père Dagobert reopened the dispute. Dagobert's tenure marks "the most shameful incident in the whole history of Louisiana, the high-handed suppression of the Jesuits in the colony," or so chastises Roger Baudier in his 1939 church-sanctioned tome, *The Catholic Church in Louisiana*.

It seems a bit overstated to heap centuries of religious infighting square on the shoulders of a frail monk, but the Capuchin friar did loudly voice his opposition to the appointment of a Jesuit priest as the new vicar-general of the Louisiana diocese. And this was just the beginning of Dagobert's obstinate stand against authority.

One popular theory holds that ghosts are restless souls seeking final closure to their lives on earth. In hindsight, perhaps, the little friar should have stuck to singing; he certainly reaped little personal benefit from raising his voice in protest. Booked for eternity to haunt a damp alley, the singing monk may provide a little impromptu entertainment for passersby, but it must be tough playing the same venue night after night.

What prompted the gentle friar to stir up such a ruckus within the Catholic Church? As the pastor of the Church of St. Louis, the first and *only* permanent Catholic church serving the residents of the port city of New Orleans, he had plenty to do. According to historian Baudier, "About this little church eddied the streams of colonial life . . . here were married those of high estate and the lowly colonists, the orphan girl from the Ursuline convent espoused to some up-river planter, the sailor, the soldier, the laborer, the slave."

The catalog of services held at the Church of St. Louis and presided over by Dagobert also included a steady round of burials where the mortal remains of "the great and the near great were . . . all borne before the sanctuary for the last prayers of Holy Mother Church before being consigned to the grave," or, for the privileged few, to the vaults below the sanctuary of the church itself.

For twenty-seven years, from 1749 to 1776, Père Dagobert de Longuory, O.M. Capuchin labored as the tenth rector of this bustling parish church in New Orleans. Although the church was modest in scale compared to the elaborate European houses of worship, its cruciform plan featured a nave 112 feet long, 32 feet wide, and 24 feet high, and it boasted, to the delight of Father Dagobert, a raised alcove dedicated to music. The original 1727 floor plans show a 10-foot space between the last pews and the front walls of the church; tucked within were a holy water font, a baptismal font, and a box for the weights for the tower clock. Floating above this area was the choir loft.

Church historians generally agree that, above all else, Dagobert was "passionately fond of church music and celebrations," singing the High Mass on Sundays and holy days of obligation. His detractors accused him of excessive vanity, spending too much time impressing the ladies with his powerful vocal range.

Dagobert also gained a dubious reputation as "The Marrying Curé." "There was not a prominent marriage in New Orleans between 1756 and the year of his death that he did not perform," pronounces Baudier. "It was also his wont to visit the homes of those just married to attend the marriage festivities"—an unheard-of practice for priests and a custom that seemed to greatly shock the more conservative Catholic religious.

It is difficult to comprehend how this "lead singer," "maker of wills," "baptizer of high and low," "defender of those in difficulty," and "friend of children" found time to become embroiled in the political/religious agenda of the day. But Père Dagobert was not simply the rector of the Church of St. Louis; he was also mindful of his responsibilities as superior of the Capuchin Order of monks for the entire Louisiana colony, stretching from the Gulf of Mexico to the Canadian provinces to the north.

Père Dagobert's brethren were spread thinly over too broad a region. Many were ill qualified; most were overworked and received little to no support from a colonial government pledged to bring civilization and the word of God to the wilderness.

One Capuchin monk, a Father Ame, was so overwhelmed he deserted his mission in Natchez. Père Dagobert jumped immediately to his defense, pointing out that Father Ame could not function, as he had neither a building for a church nor a rectory at the settlement. The church hierarchy decried this as a flimsy excuse, as "Father Ame did very wrong deserting his post . . . he should not have left unless he had fears for his life," and they intimated he lacked "the courage to offer it [his life] as a sacrifice to the state and to religion."

Note should be taken here of the priority attached to the secular needs of the state before matters of faith. For this was a time when the political agenda of kings often overrode papal decree—separation of church and state were nonexistent. Government officials wanted French missionaries to establish friendly relations with Native American tribal groups, keeping these powerful forces aligned with France. Pulling the Indians into the French Catholic fold was an excellent means to that end. The Jesuits had already established a stronghold in

Canada and demonstrated a quick facility for learning native tongues. The Capuchins did not arrive in Louisiana until 1722; they were fewer in number and not as adaptable as the Jesuits.

When Père Dagobert was informed that a Jesuit was to be made vicar-general of the Louisiana colony, he perceived this as a move to oust his Capuchin brethren, or at least make their lives more difficult. He pleaded directly to the French high court, citing letters of patent given by the king himself to the Capuchins to minister in the colony. Dagobert bypassed his lawful superior, the bishop of Quebec (who had spiritual jurisdiction over the entire Louisiana colony), aggravating an already volatile situation. The war of words dominated by charges and countercharges of incompetence, corruption, and disobedience was fought as fiercely as the physical battle between France and England during the grueling seven-year French and Indian wars.

Father Dagobert was personally attacked as unqualified for his position, but "neither his letters, nor his entries in the church records show him as ignorant," writes Baudier. "Judging by the charges leveled at him and the defense made by his supporters, he made both friends and enemies, as any unusual character will."

The religious squabbling over who had ultimate control over the souls of the Louisiana colonists and Native American tribes culminated in the ousting of the Jesuits and the temporary supremacy of the Capuchins. On July 9, 1763, the Superior Council of Louisiana, a civil court, issued an unprecedented ruling against a religious organization. The decree stated that the Jesuit missionaries were "hostile to authority" and to public peace and safety. Astonishingly, the Superior Council also declared that vows taken by the Jesuit missionaries were null and void; they were forbidden to take the name of Jesus or wear the habit of their order. The priests of the Society of Jesus, the Jesuits, were defrocked, their lands and possessions confiscated and sold at public auction. After seventy years of toiling in the New World, the Jesuits departed in disgrace.

Père Dagobert, superior of the Capuchin Order, had won. Beneath his gentle music-loving soul beat a stubborn, indefatigable will. While he did not sanction the harsh treatment of the Jesuits by the civil authorities, and in fact offered them a meal and lodgings prior to their departure, he was grateful the issue was resolved. Père Dagobert looked forward to returning to his religious duties, but there was more trouble brewing for the rector and his congregation.

Unbeknownst to the isolated Louisiana settlers, Louis XV of France had deeded their lands to his cousin, King Carlos III of Spain, through a secret treaty signed in Fontainebleau, France in 1762. When the transaction was finally revealed to the predominately French colonists in October of 1764, Père Dagobert's sympathies lay with his Creole parishioners. This French Capuchin monk was soon to become part of the legend of the "first revolutionary movement by American patriots against a European power."

The insurrection by members of Père Dagobert's congregation in 1768 predates the American Revolution of 1775 and the "shot heard round the world" at Concord, Massachusetts by seven years. Vowing never to swear allegiance to Spain, the Creoles appealed directly to France, asking to be taken back. King Louis XV was not interested, so the congregation took matters into their own hands.

Led by Nicolas Chauvin de Lafrênière, a small band of Creoles sent Don Antonio de Ulloa, the new Spanish governor, packing. Outraged by the insult to one of his officials, King Carlos of Spain ordered an army of 3,000 soldiers and twenty-four warships under Gen. Don Alexander O'Reilly to quell the revolution in New Orleans. It worked. The Creoles capitulated and offered to make peace. The Spanish general accepted their surrender, but to prove he meant business, O'Reilly had the leaders arrested, tried, and executed by firing squad.

One local legend says that the vengeful Spaniard, nicknamed "Bloody O'Reilly," ordered the five bodies of the patriots to be left to rot on the drilling grounds along the levee, downriver from the Church of St. Louis. The grieving widows pleaded to be allowed to bury their husbands. Don O'Reilly refused to grant them an audience. The widows turned to their friend, Père Dagobert.

Dagobert assembled the widows and like-minded parishioners for a special service in the church. Waiting until a foggy gray shroud enveloped the night, the nervous congregation slipped out of the side door into the alley. In a grim processional, they snatched the bodies and carried them back to the church. Père Dagobert offered a solemn requiem mass for the slain patriots. As their bodies were laid to rest, his rich baritone voice rose in a touching *Te Deum* for their souls.

History does not record General O'Reilly's reaction to this turn of events. Perhaps having made his point, he chose to ignore the body snatchers. However, on July 11, 1772, Luis de Unzaga, who replaced O'Reilly as the Spanish governor of the Louisiana province, provided an oddly favorable assessment of French Capuchin monk, Père Dagobert. "All these priests . . . are good, virtuous persons, but among them there are some who know their duties and others who do not know them very well. . . . Father Dagobert was worthy of the esteem of His Excellency Count O'Reilly, and won the admiration of all the Spaniards and because of his prudent behavior and kindness, he is loved by the people and therefore, I consider him worthy of the esteem of your Illustrious Lordship."

Either O'Reilly and Unzaga were unaware of the little monk's loyalties, or once again, Dagobert found a way to overcome insurmountable odds. The legend of Père Dagobert's role in the revolt against a foreign power does lend credence to the haunted tale of the singing monk and his affinity for the alley next to the cathedral.

After thirty-three years of service in the Louisiana colony, Père Dagobert de Longuory died on May 31, 1776, working to the very last at the old St. Louis parish church. Like his nine predecessors, he was buried in the sanctuary. Historian Baudier reports that "all New Orleans mourned him for he was greatly beloved." Father Dagobert's death symbolized the end of the era of French Capuchin missionaries in Louisiana. On Good Friday, March 21, 1788, a devastating fire in the city ravaged 856 homes and Père Dagobert's beloved Church of St. Louis. Almost six years would elapse before the charred remains were removed and a new church was erected on the site. Père Dagobert's tenacious spirit never left. His haunted concerts in the alley next to the present St. Louis Cathedral still attract a loyal following.

Tour operator Tom Duran preps his group for what he hopes will be a headline performance by "The Singing Monk." "There is a haunting within this alley that is so gentle that people do not realize they have seen something until it is too late."

Duran directs the group's attention to the cathedral's facade, where streetlights from Jackson Square cast ominous shadows over the ghostly white exterior. "One walk through the cathedral door here during the day and you will see a tablet listing the names of the priests. One from the 1770s, Père Dagobert, haunts this alley, and he appears down by the lamppost wearing his robes."

As the group enters the narrow passageway hemmed in by the cathedral to the left and the Presbytère to the right, Duran continues his warm-up act. "He looks like he could be a priest out for an evening stroll. The only time he gives it away is when he gets towards the gate and turns. He goes up those steps, and through the closed door." Duran snaps his fingers and announces, "He simply disappears!"

The consensus among other New Orleans haunted-tour guides is that the ghost of Père Dagobert appears at dusk, chanting through the long hours of the night and vanishing with the dawn. Whether his songs are still in protest over the heavy-handed practices of church and civil authorities, or are mournful prayers for redemption, time has not dampened the passionate voice of this beloved Capuchin monk.

17

The Legendary Widow Paris

Hairdresser. Voodoo priestess. Devout Catholic. Evil sorcerer. Healer. Saint or devil incarnate? True believers scoff at the idea of labels for their beloved icon. Spawning two centuries of cult-like idolatry, the Widow Paris made an astonishing impact. Her tomb in St. Louis Cemetery No. 1 is covered with grotesque graffiti-style *X* marks, etched by legions of devoted followers convinced that Marie's powers reach well beyond the grave.

There is scarcely a guidebook, history book, promotional brochure, or pamphlet on New Orleans that does not include some salute to Marie Laveau. Haunted history tours, voodoo museums, botanical stores—all capitalize on her enduring legacy. From black spiritual churches to music clubs like the House of Blues, altars to this voodoo priestess are a formidable testament to her abiding presence. If ever there was an argument for the ability of spirits of the dead to commune with the living, it is embodied in Marie Laveau. Her powers were linked inexorably to her ability to sway (some say blackmail) others. With little or no recorded education, Marie parlayed her gifted, almost telepathic, insight of the human condition into a profitable business venture. This consummate showman offered up symbolic voodoo rituals (for a price) as the panacea for life's ailments. And while Marie did not invent voodoo, she was its most charismatic proponent.

The enigmatic Marie was born in 1794 (some researchers place this date as early as 1783, others as late as the 1820s). Clouding the issue is Marie's namesake, a daughter who also practiced a form of voodoo under the name Marie Laveau. The second Marie was not averse to promulgating the myth that she was the reincarnation of her mother, giving rise to the belief that the original Marie remained eternally youthful.

Although Marie sometimes claimed she was the daughter of a French nobleman and his octoroon mistress, Barbara Rosendale Duggal, in an essay for Sybil Kein's *Creole: The History and Legacy of Louisiana's Free People of Color,* cites a recently uncovered document that helps to define Marie's origins. On August 4, 1819, Père Antoine, rector of St. Louis Cathedral in New Orleans, officiated at the marriage of Santiago Paris and Marie Labeau (better known as Jacques Paris and Marie Laveau; variations in spelling and French adaptations of Spanish surnames were common in Creole Louisiana). The Notarial Records also list both of Marie's parents, Margarita D'arcantel and Carlos Labeau, as free people of color. Despite myths circulated by Marie Laveau herself, and writers who magnified her deeds, there is scant proof that Marie was a descendant of French nobility.

Marie's parents were seemingly well established at the time of their daughter's wedding. Carlos Labeau (also listed in the *National Trust Guide* as Charles Laveaux) gives the young couple a small cottage in the 1900 block of Rampart Street.

Marie and Jacques (Santiago), a carpenter by trade, lead a quiet life; there is no mention of children or dabbling in the occult. Jacques dies (or disappears) a few years later and Marie assumes the title of *Veuve* (Widow) Paris, the name that appears on the tombstone in St. Louis Cemetery No. 1.

At the age of thirty-two, the Widow Paris is a ravishing beauty; flaunting her luminous eyes and thick curls of black hair, she forms a tempestuous liaison with the equally attractive

Capt. Christophe Duminy Glapion. This lasting union results in fifteen children. To support her growing family, Marie works as a hairdresser. On the surface, she is no different from others in the community of *personnes de couleur libres* who live and thrive in nineteenth-century New Orleans.

Unlike the overeager Chloe at The Myrtles Plantation, caught and punished for eavesdropping on private conversations, Marie the hairdresser is the epitome of discretion, carefully pocketing each personal morsel her wealthy clients unwittingly drop. As she arranges their elaborate coifs in the sanctity of their boudoirs, the relaxed mademoiselles literally and figuratively let their hair down. Chattering incessantly, they leave unguarded the doors to their innermost thoughts and desires. Marie, the choreographer of human emotions, takes her cue and offers to help the teary-eyed damsel snare her wavering gentleman caller or find revenge for a broken heart.

Passing the whispered secrets of one client into the waiting ears of another, Marie, the master chess player, moves her kings, queens, and pawns about the board, setting up Creole society in endless scenarios of check and checkmate. For special effect Marie, the sorcerer, devises *gris-gris,* magic concoctions of nail clippings and strands of hair mingled with brick dust, then wadded and tied in small bundles of cloth. As rumors of her success mount, her stature increases. Sometime between 1826 and her recorded death on June 16, 1881, Marie Laveau emerges as the most widely regarded and feared Queen of Voodoo.

In *Marie Laveau, Voodoo Queen,* author Raymond J. Martinez recounts a particularly convoluted saga where the Widow Paris is credited with masterminding fate.

A dissolute son of a prominent New Orleans family takes advantage of an innocent young girl. The girl's father races to the police, who charge the attacker with rape. Public sentiment rises against the young man and his attorney is less than confident of his client's chances. In a panic, the young man contacts Marie Laveau and pleads for help. He tells her his father will pay her anything she wants if she will arrange for an acquittal.

Shortly before the trial, the young man informs his father he has sought Marie's assistance. The father is incredulous, but promises that if she can keep his son out of jail he will give her a house he owns on St. Ann Street in the Quarter. Just before daybreak on the first day of the trial, Marie slips into the courtroom and places a concoction of herbs (one version claims it is three Guinea peppers) under the judge's desk. She also goes to the judge's home, where she places another bag of gris-gris on his front porch with a signed note saying, The boy is innocent.

At this juncture in her career, Marie relies on intimidation as much as any magic potions, for no one wants to cross the all-powerful Voodoo Queen of New Orleans.

Marie's imposing figure dominates the courtroom. Her hair, piled high, is caught in a tignon, a scarf striped with burgundy and sky blue—a fitting crown for a high priestess. Her shoulders, royally draped with a matching burgundy fringed shawl, are rigid; deep-set eyes stare ominously at the judge. As the prosecuting attorney argues vehemently for the maximum penalty for the young man's outrageous crime, Marie takes aim. Making a great show of plucking a long strand of her dark hair and wrapping it in a piece of paper, she casually flicks the wadded ball at the lawyer. It bounces off his shoulder, landing on the table in front of him. Those present cannot swear it causes the attorney to halt his speech, but it is at precisely that moment he chooses to conclude his remarks. The jury returns with a verdict of not guilty and Marie receives her house as payment for services rendered.

The fact that the young man on trial is judged by a jury of his peers—fellow playboys whose past indiscretions must put a certain prejudicial slant on their deliberations—is conveniently ignored.

In Act II of this drama, the acquitted young man begins to exhibit signs of remorse for his unwarranted attack. He avoids his old crowd and becomes a familiar figure at church.

One morning at mass, he sees his innocent victim kneeling in prayer (we shall call her Doucette to protect her privacy). He kneels beside her and begs her forgiveness. Doucette flees the church in fear. Our young friend (again, for reasons of privacy, we shall call him Charles) is determined to right the wrong and marry the beautiful Doucette. Charles is clearly in need of help, so it's back to Marie for a little more voodoo. For an undisclosed fee, the Voodoo Queen whips up a love potion.

Laveau biographer Raymond Martinez must have some inside information, for he catalogs the ingredients to be worn by Charles in a pouch around his waist as "love powder . . . feathers, pulverized lizard eggs, and the hair of a jackass." How such repugnant aromas would boost Charles' chances is known only to Marie. Adding to the questionable hygiene practices, Marie also sprinkles Doucette's doorstep with Charles' hair taken from "various parts of his body." Charles puts his trust, and his body, in Marie's hands, dutifully wearing his odoriferous gris-gris pouch. After a month of patient waiting at the church, he gets close enough to speak to Doucette.

Now, whether she catches a whiff of Charles' rancid odor, or she is still frightened by the very sight of him, Doucette spins around a mite too fast, stumbles, and sprains her ankle. The gallant Charles rushes to her rescue and begs to be allowed to pick her up and carry her to the doctor.

Act III finds a newly solicitous (and hopefully bathed) Charles attending to Doucette at home.

Encouraged by her smile, he asks on bended knee for her hand in marriage. Doucette is so impressed by his transformation, she agrees to marry him, limping all the way to the altar.

The curtain rings down on this happy ending courtesy of the talented Marie Laveau.

G. William Nott in a 1922 article for the *New Orleans Times-Picayune* relates the same basic story; he quotes an "octogenarian mammy" who swears such happy endings are proof that Marie Laveau was a not a "wicked woman" and used her powers only for good and charitable causes.

Layers of legendary and outlandish feats have both venerated and obliterated the real Marie Laveau. Eyewitnesses insisted she kept a twenty-foot-long venomous snake named Zombi in an alabaster box, who feasted on "fair and tender children"; she presided over Calinda dances in Congo Square (in present-day Armstrong Park) and bacchanalian voodoo rites held near a shack on Bayou St. John. As the reigning Voodoo Queen, Marie led the dancing, where she wriggled naked with her serpent (this must have been quite a sight as the very fertile Marie was perpetually pregnant).

Her rituals as reported by author Martinez were "so outrageously vulgar that children were forbidden to witness them," and respectable adults attended in disguise so as not to be branded as proponents of depravity. Marie, dressed like a gypsy with rings on her fingers and ears (there is no mention of bells on her toes), alternated drinking prodigious amounts of tafia (a potent mixture of molasses and rum) with sucking blood, vampire style, from live chickens and cats. Marie could also conjure and foretell the future. She reigned as the ultimate witch, casting spells and hexes. Apparently the only thing Marie did not do was grab a *broom* and fly over the spires of the cathedral.

Exactly how and when Marie, baptized and married in the Catholic religion, was first drawn to voodoo is unknown. From the time the French explorer LaSalle laid claim to the Louisiana Territory in 1682, the prevailing religion of the Louisiana colony was Catholicism. The *Code Noir,* the Black Code, instituted in 1724, mandated that all slaves be baptized in the Roman Catholic faith. New Orleans' third strata of citizenry, free people of color, walked a fine line between the white and black populace. There were several avenues through which a slave could attain the elevated status of *les gens de couleur libres,* explains Mary Gehman in her work *The Free People of Color of New Orleans:* a slave could be granted his freedom by his master (usually at the master's death), buy his freedom, be born into it as the second generation of a free black, or have entered the Louisiana colony from the Caribbean as an already free person. Outwardly, free blacks also adhered to the rituals and sacraments of the Catholic Church. But behind curtained doorways, many clung to the traditional beliefs of the voodoo spirit world.

Many West African slaves, primarily members of the Dahomey, Yoruba and Konga tribes, and free people of color like Marie's parents arrived in New Orleans from Haiti. Originally captured by the French in the late eighteenth century, the enslaved people were transported to the western half of the island of Haiti (then known as Saint Domingue) to work the sugarcane fields.

Meeting clandestinely at night, rebellious slaves gathered solace, strength, and inspiration from their native religion. Voudou practitioners believed that each animate and inanimate object in nature had a spirit double, a ghost. When a man or creature died, his ghost remained close by. In times of need, a person could call on these spirits.

As stories of slave revolts were passed on, Marie became aware that no one had more successfully wielded supernatural forces for protection than the masterful rebel leader Toussaint L'Overture. To instill his rebel forces with confidence, he relied on Haiti's powerful Voudou priests; in the great slave rebellions of 1769 and 1791, these priests conjured up ghosts to guard the slaves from their white masters. L'Overture was instrumental in establishing Haiti as the first black republic in the Americas.

Somewhere between the pulsating drumbeats, the rhythmic chanting, and the whispered legends, Marie put aside the more staid rites of Catholicism and embraced ancient tribal ways. Philip M. Hannan, the retired eleventh Catholic archbishop (1965-88) of the diocese of New Orleans, is familiar with Marie's checkered history. "Marie Laveau, of course she was married in the Church. Everybody has a right to be married in the Church. She was a Catholic, a practicing Catholic." Having claimed her as part of the fold, Archbishop Hannan immediately inserts a qualifier to his validation of Marie's faith: "But that doesn't mean she didn't go wrong."

Even if Marie Laveau had heard such a judgment during her lifetime, she would have paid little heed. On a quest to discover her spiritual roots, she learned that the spirit world of the West African animist was governed by a supreme god often preoccupied with the cosmic forces of the universe. Therefore, much like any other bureaucratic hierarchy, there existed in the sacred arts of Haitian Voudou a level of subdeities called *loas,* each with its own specialty like Legba, the protector of homes, and Domballah, the serpent god. These individual *loas* were accorded different physical traits, and they granted favors based on offerings of favorite foods and drinks. The highly intuitive Widow Paris understood that those who successfully communicated with these *loas* were credited with possessing the power to influence others.

Most importantly, Marie learned that to practice Voudou in Catholic New Orleans would require a degree of ingenuity; voodoo, as the Haitian religion came to be known in the Crescent City, was considered a form of "pagan devil worship." By 1782 the good white Catholic citizens of New Orleans so feared the "evil forces" of voodoo, they sought to ban "this abomination." Rituals that invoked spirits of the dead were both sacrilegious and frightening. Slaves outnumbered their white masters; any gathering of slaves in or around the city was cause for concern for it might lead to revolt.

Cleverly deflecting the adverse reaction to voodoo, Marie used the Catholic symbols of holy water, incense, candles, and statues of the saints as perfect foils for various voodoo effigies, fetishes, and ceremonies. Her brand of voodoo was like a three-ring circus with the Widow Paris as ringmaster. She strad-dled both religions so well it was impossible to discern her true allegiance.

When one of hairdresser Marie's clients falls sobbing in her arms, dev-astated on learning of her husband's affair with his quadroon mistress, Marie hints there might be a way to cure him of his wandering ways.

At first the proper Creole lady moans she could never dabble in the occult.

Marie responds, "You pray to your saints for help, do you not, madame? Are they not good spirits ready to render assistance? In voodoo, we pray to spirits too including Saint Barbara; we ask for their guidance and intercession. Sometimes it is difficult to reach them, but they have left us remedies and cures, if only we believe."

How can madame resist the kind offer of help from Marie? Marie is Catholic too. Are not all her children baptized in St. Louis Cathedral? Does Marie not carry a crucifix? Does she not believe in God? Has Marie not helped other women in her position? What are a few gold coins, if not to buy happiness?

A small packet of gris-gris levitates from Marie's basket into madame's hands.

The offending quadroon mistress wakens to find a double black cross etched outside her front door.

Madame's husband is immediately informed by his panicked mistress that their "pleasant interludes" are over.

When the astute husband realizes that the clever plot is orchestrated by Marie, he seeks her out. "Have you heard I am being considered for a very important political position? My worthy opponent has been looking a little pale. Perhaps you might know of a cure for his illness?"

Marie's little basket of goodies holds one less potion.

Ron Bodin, author of *Voodoo, Past and Present*, attributes the following to voodoo priestess Marie Laveau:

> To harm an enemy, write his name on a slip of paper, then put the paper in the mouth of a snake. Hang the snake in the sun to dry. As the snake suffers and dies, so will your enemy succumb to the same slow, agonizing death.

Whether Marie provided the snake is unclear—perhaps for a small extra fee.

Although she amassed large sums of money, Marie, her common-law husband, Christophe Glapion, and their fifteen children lived frugally for nearly fifty years in an unassuming cottage in the French Quarter, the same cottage she had received as a gift from the grateful father of the errant young man.

The humble dwelling on St. Ann Street may have been part of the act, for Marie, the high priestess, was ever mindful of her image and her flock. Creole gentlemen and ladies were her main source of income; they might secretly attend her voodoo ceremonies to be titillated by the masses whipped into frenzied orgies. Yet Marie remained keenly in tune to her true congregation—poor slaves, free mulattos, quadroons, and octoroons. The backyard of her cottage witnessed a daily parade of common folk seeking cures, incantations, and divinations.

Like a modern-day evangelist, Marie used the media to get her message to the people. Her annual St. John's Eve (June 23) extravaganza, held on the banks of Bayou St. John near Lake Pontchartrain, was equal parts religious fervor, hedonistic exhibition, and business enterprise. The carnival-like atmosphere included the selling of charms and magic potions. As much as people complained about the lewd behavior, the sacrificial slaughter of animals, and the noise, the police rarely interfered—many owed their good fortunes to a favor from Marie.

The press flocked to report on the sensational event, open to all comers (for a fee, of course). Trembling, swooning, and falling into a trance, scantily clad young men and women danced to hypnotic drumbeats around a bonfire blazing through the summer night. Many passed out from a lethal combination of whiskey and heat exhaustion.

Marie was also said to have led her flock in the Lord's Prayer and the singing of Christian hymns, all the while holding Zombi, her serpent, aloft. In Haitian Voudou, *zombi* has a particularly evil connotation. A *zombi* is a soulless human corpse taken from the grave and transformed into a living creature— a gruesome version of "Dead Man Walking." Church officials condemned Marie's conduct as "blasphemous," but the notoriety only added to her appeal.

In Marie's later years, her eccentric behavior included visiting condemned prisoners moments before their execution. Some point to this as proof of Marie's goodness—comforting those who were about to make their final journey. As evidence they cite *The Daily Picayune* dated May 10, 1871: "For more than twenty years, whenever a human being has suffered the final penalty in the Parish Prison, an old colored woman has come to their cell and prepared an altar for them. This woman is Marie Levau [*sic*], better known as a Priestess of the Voudous."

The reporter goes on to describe a typical altar erected by Marie: "It consists of a box about three feet square; above this are three pyramidal boxes raising to a small apex on which is placed a small figure of the Virgin. The altar is draped in white . . . in the center rests a prayerbook in Spanish, and behind it two angels with wings outspread . . . the veil of the Virgin is beautifully wrought and ornamented with flowers." There is no mention of voodoo symbols.

The verdict remains in limbo on whether Marie gave up voodoo entirely in her latter years in favor of Catholicism. Many suspect that her prayer sessions with the condemned were her way of doing a little advanced scouting for the time when she too would cross over to the other side. Marie's passing occurred on June 16, 1881. Her obituary in *The Daily Picayune,* titled "The Death of Marie Laveau," stated simply, "At 5 o'clock yesterday evening Marie Laveau was buried in her family tomb in St. Louis Cemetery."

In many black spiritual churches around New Orleans (notably those with women bishops), Marie Laveau continues to be revered and called upon to act as a spirit guide. Ava Kay Jones, one of the most active voodoo and Yoruba priestesses in the United States, credits Marie with bringing the secret practice of voodoo out into the open. Jones, an accredited attorney, attempts to clarify misconceptions about voodoo, which she feels has gotten a bad rap. Voodoo, says Jones, is not devil worship and is not intent on causing pain or suffering. She states that the word voodoo is derived from a Fon word (from the Dahomey people in West Africa) and means spirit or deity, with no evil or immoral connotation.

Others, like Archbishop E. J. Johnson of the Israelite Divine Black Spiritual Church, condemn Marie and her followers as "worshipers of Satan." Clad in scarlet robes, the ninety-plus-year-old Archbishop Johnson has just finished playing the organ for a Sunday service in his altar-bedecked church. In a voice cracking with age, he recalls his grandmother and the perils of slavery. "My daddy's mother was a slave of Jefferson Davis [the president of the Confederacy]. . . . When they were freed, they came down to New Orleans on a riverboat." Waving a finger in warning, Johnson cautions against the evils of voodoo. "People like that will do you harm. . . . I remember times when I was younger, those people [voodoo practitioners] . . . I've known them to take dolls, make black dolls and stick pins and needles in them, and put them in a shoebox, and put them on your porch with a note saying, 'You're going to die at such and such a time.' And it would frighten people to death . . . it really would cause them to die."

As you enter St. Louis Cemetery No. 1 on Basin Street behind the French Quarter, the sun bounces harshly off the whitewashed tombs. To the left of the main entrance, near the wall vaults, stands the most visited tomb in all of New Orleans. It is tall and narrow, plaster over brick, with a pitched roof and three tiers of vertical chambers. The inscription reads:

Famille Vve. Paris,
née Laveau
Ci-Git
Marie Philomen Glapion
decédée le 11 Juin 1897
agée de soixante-deux ans
Elle fut bonne mère, bonne amie et
regrettée par tous ceux qui l'ont connue
Passants priez pour elle.

(Family of the Widow Paris, born Laveau. Here lies Marie Philomen Glapion died on June 11, 1897 at the age of sixty-two. She was a good mother, good friend, and lamented by all those who knew her. Passersby pray for her.)

Robert Florence in his *City of the Dead*, a literary journey through this venerable resting place, points out that the date of death on the tomb, 1897, corresponds with Marie's daughter's demise and raises the question of who is buried here. As is the custom in New Orleans, single tombs accept multiple burials—

many generations of the same family share cramped quarters. Marie Laveau, the mother, could be interred within, but, speculates Florence, if she was, her remains were probably removed. Crumbled bones, especially those of a prominent voodoo queen, Florence explains, "are one of the most popular forms of gris-gris."

Cemetery guard Allen Lee watches in amazement as young people in full Gothic regalia—black clothes, purple lips, pierced body parts—bump into middle-age couples in shorts and sandals, all jockeying to tap into the Voodoo Queen's supernatural powers. "All they want to know is, where is Marie's tomb?" says the astonished guard.

On any given day, bizarre offerings are laid at the base of the tomb: purple Mardi Gras beads wrapped around the neck of a dead rat, slices of stale cake and French bread, black votive candles, an unopened bottle of Voodoo beer, a string of white plastic rosary beads. The Catholic Archdiocese of New Orleans, which owns and maintains the cemetery grounds, must make a daily sweep of these "tributes" to the Voodoo Queen.

The final abode of the Laveau/Paris/Glapion families is also marred by a blanket of *X* marks covering every square inch. The custom of making a wish at Marie's tomb has been perpetuated by a nonstop convoy of tour guides. These misguided tour operators instruct their customers to perform a series of hokey-pokey gyrations that have little in common with voodoo: "Take a piece of brick and make three *X*s. Knock three times to get the attention of the spirits. Tap the tomb with your foot, then scrape the ground three times, bow, turn to the left to banish negativity, and bow again." After a final turn back to the right, the discombobulated tourist is told, "Marie is ready to grant your wish."

Glapion family members, Marie Laveau's descendants who have legal ownership of the tomb, are offended by the desecration and graffiti. Just a few paces away, in stark contrast to the vandalized gravesite, the neighboring tomb is pristine. Adorned with a simple white cross, it is the final resting place of another powerful local figure, Ernest ("Dutch") Morial, the first African-American mayor of New Orleans, and father of the current mayor, Marc Morial. If Marie is still around, she must enjoy the irony of sharing eternity with the very Catholic and politically connected former mayor.

No matter what the controversy over who may, or may not, be buried in the popular tomb in St. Louis Cemetery No. 1, to voodoo practitioners the site is a shrine to a compelling woman whose protective spirit will always hover over the city of her birth.

18

Celtic Love Triangle

Carried by waves of Irish immigrants from the 1840s through the 1860s, Celtic legends arrived in New Orleans, adding to the port city's mystique. While some might find it odd to discover an authentic Irish pub in the heart of the French Quarter, the haunting ballads that are the hallmarks of Irish culture offer the perfect balm for three spirits who claim this entertaining spot as their own. Angelique, Joseph and Mary form a ghostly triumvirate that has refused to be "cleared" from the property.

Entrance to O'Flaherty's Irish Channel Pub on the first block of Toulouse Street is through a brick-lined arched carriage way joining two historic buildings. Ducking under a sea of flags representing the seven Celtic nations—Ireland, Scotland, Wales, Cornwall, the Isle of Man, Brittany, and Galicia—visitors are intrigued to find themselves in a charming Spanish-style courtyard complete with a triple-tiered fountain. When Irish balladeer Danny O'Flaherty went shopping in 1985 for a site for his new music club, the combination of the courtyard fountain and historic buildings proved irresistible. "It looked like Galway City; it reminded me of home—the doors, the windows, the arches are just like some of the Spanish architecture in Galway," affirms the transplanted

Irishman. Danny grew up with his sisters and brothers in the rugged Gaeltecht region of western Ireland, where myths of fairies and leprechauns still exert a powerful hold over the land and its people.

Preoccupied with transforming the circa-1800 New Orleans complex into a pub and restaurant, Danny was unaware at first that his long-term lease included a built-in audience of troubled spirits. Given a choice of which ghost he'd rather play for, Danny favors Angelique. "Angelique, God bless her, she watches us play music. Now I haven't seen her myself because I can't be looking upstairs and singing all the time, but my staff tells me that everytime I sing certain songs, she appears. In that way, we've gotten to know each other very well."

When not on tour, Danny O'Flaherty and The Celtic Folk play weekend nights in the Ballad Room, a special performance venue to the right of the main entrance. The ceiling of the Ballad Room has been cut out, exposing the timbered beams of the second-floor entresol level. From this high vantage point, the diaphanous apparition of Angelique peers down over the heads of the performers and the audience. As Danny reaches into his back left pocket to pull out a tin whistle, Angelique settles in. The lilting notes from Danny's Irish flute weave their own magic spell, holding the fragile figure captive. Her sighs are palpable, for Danny's soulful rendition of a traditional Scottish ballad rekindles the pain of her lover's betrayal. "If my true love she were gone, I would surely find another. Where wild mountain thyme grows, around the blooming heather, will ye go, lassie, go?" The lyrics usually prove too much for the tenderhearted Angelique. Smiling sadly at the Irish balladeer below, she takes her leave.

Repeated complaints—from his bartenders, waitresses, family, and friends—of ghostly interruptions, both gentle and rude, forced the singer/songwriter to dig into the matter. Danny headed straight for the Historic New Orleans Collection, a vast repository of information about the city and its inhabitants.

From 1722 to 1795, the property passed through a series of owners. Intrigued by his research, Danny discovers an advertisement dated August 21, 1802: *For Sale. A house situated in the street of the Government House [Toulouse Street] built of brick and roofed with tiles . . . there are in the said house a store . . . two fine apartments . . . a brick kitchen on which is an upper story. Apply to M. Bastien Estevan, proprietor, who lives there.* Reading between the notarial lines, it is clear to the Irish bard that the next recorded act of sale set in motion the haunted love triangle.

On March 3, 1803, Don Guillaume Marre affixes his name to the deed. Don Guillaume has recently wed a stunning widow, Mary Wheaton Sevre of Cumberland, New Jersey. Three years later, a notation dated October 13, 1806, reveals that the aforementioned widow, Mary Wheaton Sevre, is now sole owner of the property by virtue of the death of her second husband, Don Guillaume Marre. The widow Marre wasted no time in picking out husband number three, Joseph Baptandiere, native of Aute Luce, Mont Blanc, France. In marrying Joseph, the merry widow Mary apparently met her match.

Reared in the small fishing village of Connemara outside of Galway, Danny O'Flaherty learned from an early age to trust his instincts, and his instincts told him the hauntings somehow centered on the marrying Mary. "I think probably that every tribe that God has created is very superstitious, but Irish beliefs are very unique." In a heavy brogue that colors his speech with the wild beauty of the Emerald Isle, Danny speaks of an ancient landscape populated by Celts, Druids, and little people. "You know, I can take any nonbeliever back to Ireland during the winter and I tell you, it wouldn't take more than forty-eight hours for he or she to be afraid of the landscape at nightime . . . there's something about the air, the surroundings in Ireland that's different than any other place in the world. I don't know whether we're more or less superstitious than anybody else, but I think probably that there are *things* living there, and we see them."

What Danny saw when he read of the marriage between

Mary and Joseph, husband number three, was trouble. And the trouble arrived in the dark Creole beauty of Angelique.

In late eighteenth- and early nineteenth-century New Orleans, there was a common practice known as *plaçage*; this arrangement involved wealthy white, often married, gentlemen and free women of color, *demoiselles de couleur.* Author Mary Gehman explains in *The Free People of Color of New Orleans* that these liaisons often lasted a lifetime and the women involved viewed themselves as their white protectors' "other" wives. A woman living in such an arrangement was a *placée,* from the French "placed"; her benefactor usually set her up with a house and slaves of her own.

As Danny O'Flaherty was to discover, Angelique Dubois and Joseph Baptandiere had entered into a mutually beneficial mode of *plaçage*. But, there was a hitch. Angelique was madly in love with Joseph and desired to be his real wife. Joseph had managed to keep his liaison with Angelique from Mary, who he knew from experience was not one to look the other way. The inevitable happened.

There is nothing like a bewitching curly-haired, blue-eyed bard to lift a love triangle gone awry to the level of epic prose, but such is the consummate skill of one Daniel J. O'Flaherty. "One day they were having a rout [Danny transforms this one-syllable euphemism for "fight" into an entire nine-round boxing match] and Angelique said she was going to tell on him to Mary, his wife. And he didn't know how to take it. And I believe he strangled her to death; he killed her. And he buried Angelique in the courtyard." Danny indicates a small raised spot in the garden lining the rear wall. Nearby, couples sip their drinks in the peaceful courtyard under a canopy of trees strung with miniature lights, unaware of Angelique's final abode.

However, on the night of the murder, there was a witness. "This little teenage boy saw him digging the grave, and Joseph saw the boy. So he knew the cat was out of the bag and he couldn't face Mary. He went up to the third floor, put a rope around his neck, and jumped off the building. And ever since then, his spirit has never left." Empathizing with the woeful ghost of Joseph, Danny declares, "He can be very grouchy. If I jumped off the third floor, I'd be grouchy myself, whether I was living or dead."

Today the third floor of the Creole townhouse is used for storage of odds and ends. The wide-plank floors are covered in dust and pitted with holes; the brick fireplaces are barren, stripped of their cypress mantels. O'Flaherty's employees reluctantly venture up to the third level only to untangle a Celtic flag trapped in the balcony railings outside the former master bedroom.

Danny's siblings are also adamant about avoiding the upper floors of their brother's pub. "My sisters won't go up on the third floor at all anymore," says Danny. "Ann Marie once went up there and saw Angelique, and Kathleen heard strange noises on the third floor. You know it's no wonder Ann Marie went back to Ireland and Kathleen is in Chicago. They left me and my brother Patrick by ourselves."

There is some debate about which ghost is going out of his/her way to frighten people off. The murder/suicide of Angelique and Joseph happened in 1810. The disposition of Mary Wheaton Sevre Marre Baptandiere's will took place in probate court on March 15, 1817.

A few of the regular patrons at O'Flaherty's talk about a spirit who rattles around the buildings throwing temper tantrums. They believe it's the jealous Mary, still in a rage over her husband's affair with Angelique. In one extreme instance, books flew off of the shelves in the Celtic Gift Shop, located in the service building at the rear of the courtyard. The angry ghost seemed to be aiming at an attractive female customer who had the misfortune of entering the shop at an inopportune moment. As the story makes the rounds at the bar, the regulars down their glasses of Guinness in the familiar "I-told-you-so camaraderie" of ones who have seen it all before.

Wrapped in the embrace of "Ol' Man River," the Crescent City nurtures a love of exotic cultures and characters that is insatiable. When word got out that the Irish pub on Toulouse Street was haunted, ghost tours flocked to O'Flaherty's. A Japanese film crew camped out overnight, attempting to be the first to capture the ghosts in action. The syndicated television show "Strange Universe" aired feature stories (shot by photographer Oak Lea) on the paranormal phenomena at the pub, and budding parapsychologists poured through, hoping to experience a psychic encounter.

But the ghost business and the music business began to hit a few sour notes. "I thought the ghosts were going to go on strike because of the way people were fighting over them," stated Danny in the midst of the fray. The competition for rights to call on O'Flaherty's ghosts was also wreaking havoc on the pub's paying customers. As more and more haunted-tour guides arrived with their groups in tow and blockaded the courtyard, Celtic music fans were jostled aside. Danny's older brother Patrick, himself a fine musician, indeed known as "the finest mandolin player on the planet," had enough.

Things came to a head when haunted-tour guides complained that the music from the Ballad Room and the Informer Pub was disturbing their psychic connections with the ghosts. The ghost guides demanded absolute silence when they laid their hands on the "cold" spot in the courtyard over Angelique's grave. Negotiations for a peaceful resolution between musicians and ghost hunters failed; the ghost tours were banned from O'Flaherty's.

Times-Picayune newspaper columnist Christopher Rose compared the battle over which haunted-tour business had the inside track to a specific ghost to "a real-life game of Dungeons and Dragons." Rose's article, "The Invasion of the Tourist Snatchers," captured the frenzy erupting in the lucrative ghost industry. "There is no shortage of go-cup-clutching middle Americans eager to plop down $15 to hear tales of the city's dark and lusty past."

To ensure that no other tour group could profit from the haunted spirits at O'Flaherty's, one enterprising parapsychologist performed what he called a "clearing" on the property. He announced in his company's newsletter that "from a scientific point of view it is unfortunate to no longer have such a laboratory [to provide] valuable data to aid in the field of Paranormal research." O'Flaherty's ghosts were declared to have vacated the premises—*personae non gratae.* In short, if the parapsychologist's company couldn't have access to the spirits of the dead at the pub, then with a little skilled sorcery, no one else could either.

Meanwhile, Danny O'Flaherty had a surprise announcement of his own. It seems that after the psychic clearing, Angelique, Joseph, and Mary took a little trip. A couple of hundred years of haunting the same venue proved a little tiresome. Seeking a change of pace, they flitted about, checking out other music clubs around the globe. But lo and behold, declares the mischievous Irishman, they missed the cozy ambiance of his Irish pub and . . . "they're baaack!"

For Danny O'Flaherty the whole issue of ghosts is really quite simple. "There are two ways of looking at it—you can live with them, or you can be afraid the rest of your life." And with wry humor O'Flaherty slips in, "If you can get a happy medium, you're in great shape."

Like a skilled stepdancer, Danny O'Flaherty does a lively jig hopping over controversial issues and smoothing the waters. He would prefer not to offend anyone, but there are certain traditions, ceremonies, and symbols this true son of the old country will never be without. Besides the requisite St. Patrick's Day shenanigans and decorations, a currach (in local parlance, an Irish pirogue or rowing skiff) is strapped permanently to the ceiling over the bar, and the walls are emblazoned with shields bearing the coats of arms of the counties in Ireland. The establishment is opened each day with a ritual page turning of the *Book of Kells,* which is locked in a special alcove under the stairs. Steaming plates of shepherd's pie and Irish stew are mainstays on the menu, and Celtic folk tunes—jigs, sea chanteys, ballads, hornpipes, and reels—are the only music allowed. As proof that the old ways live, Danny also insists on observing Celtic New Year, Samhain, on Halloween.

The ancient Celtic calendar marked the eve of October 31 through the dawning of November 1 as the high Feast of Samhain (rhymes with *cow*-in). This was the most important time in the Celtic year as winter and summer were the two defining seasons. Thus Samhain ("Sam"—end of; "hain"—summer) marked the end of the old year and the beginning of the new. It was also a time of great personal danger, for in the waning hours of October 31, it was believed that the barriers between the natural and supernatural worlds were lowered and the creatures of the other world were free to roam, visible to mankind.

"During Samhain, it's the closest you can be to the dead. On October 31 the dead can come back and visit—sit in your living room, if they want." And just as you would do for any company, "food would be laid out for them, for the dead, and we do it every Celtic New Year's Eve here at O'Flaherty's as well," explains the generous Mr. O'Flaherty. "We put tables full of food in the courtyard and we talk to the dead, or you can talk to someone in the family that came before you. And we wish them well. It's an old Celtic custom." It is little wonder that Angelique, Joseph, and Mary came back—a roof over their heads, music *and* food in abundance. That's pretty good service for a trio of ghosts.

O'Flaherty, the Irish impresario, does offer a few words of caution to those who set out to lure ghosts to their table. Spirits of the dead and other mystical creatures possess extraordinary powers on October 31 and are particularly fond of tricking humans. In Ireland, "fairies can be pretty mean," says Danny. "They would abduct you, kidnap you, and take you to their mounds, where you would be trapped forever." So the O'Flaherty children learned, like others in their village, to try and disguise themselves that night. "If you were wearing a coat, for instance, you turn the coat inside out so they wouldn't rec-ognize you. Or if you're standing on some kind of dirt, you get that dirt underneath your shoes and you throw it at them and they would leave you alone. Us little wee ones, we were afraid, and I'll put it to you this way, there wasn't many people in my village that would go out that night because you might meet your relative that was gone before you. So people would light a candle for their deceased loved ones in their house—or those that were brave would put the candle on the grave where the person had died."

Listening to Danny lay out the past is like embarking on a breathless voyage through time. The centuries peel away. You're standing on the jagged cliffs of the Aran Islands; the sea is battering the shoreline. Bonfires are lit to encourage the warmth of the sun and hold back the darkness of the coming winter months. All about you, children in coarse shapeless robes the color of the earth are scrambling for more peat for the bonfires.

To confuse and frighten off the dead emerging from their dank graves, the adults don animal skins, wave sticks above their heads, and growl ferociously. Others are carving out turnips to hold a flicker of light from the bonfire. As they fashion these portable torches, the light catches and eerie faces grin from the hollowed-out roots. It is only with the arrival of the pink-seared dawn that the Druid families relax their guard. The old year has been laid to rest, the dead have returned to their graves, and the ancient Celts greet the new year with a collective sigh of relief—the Feast of Samhain is over.

Back in the present, you realize with startling clarity that Halloween is not just some make-believe children's game played out in Kmart plastic costumes and candy trick-or-treat scavenger hunts. The Celtic Feast of Samhain never died; it was just conveniently appropriated. Early Christian leaders found it was far easier to change the meaning of a celebration than to eliminate it. The 31st of October was dubbed All Souls' Day and declared a hallowed evening. The dawn of the first day of the Celtic New Year, November 1, was transformed into All Saints' Day.

Fr. William Maestri, a Catholic moral theologian, sums up the Christian sleight-of-hand conversion of Halloween. "What you have here on All Saints' Day and All Souls' Day, especially All Souls' Day, is the great Catholic genius of 'if there's something good about it, we'll grab it, baptize it, claim it as our own, and claim we invented it.'" With his gray hair cropped to within a half-inch of his scalp, a complexion so fair it defies description, and a skeletal frame wrapped in an innocuous black shirt and trousers, Father Maestri demands your undivided attention, for you fear if you look away for even the briefest instant, he will simply dissolve into particles of dust. Then his blue-gray eyes home in and this dynamic personality cuts through layers of dogma. "Catholics talk about all saints, whom we remember as all the good dead who have died, and we celebrate them and keep their memory alive because we believe they're with God anyway. And secondly, all souls, we pray for all of those who have died, that they may ultimately reside in the mercy of God. *Not* that they're going to be sent back to us. *Not* that they're going to make contact. . . . Ultimately what we want for them is we want them to rest in peace. . . . What you have in the idea of Halloween and these kinds of things is a human attempt to take the terror out of death. And how do you do it? Well, you make a costume. You make it a ritual. Ritual is one way we control the uncontrollable."

Christian-centuries later, Power Rangers, Superman, and Xena, Princess Warrior costumes replace animal skins, plastic jack-o'-lanterns and pumpkins have taken over for the turnip torches, and hordes of children out trick or treating are a less threatening version of the hijinks instigated by kidnapping fairies. The modern celebration of Halloween remains the only true Celtic holiday observed without interruption through the ebb and flow of time.

And at a certain Irish pub in the heart of New Orleans' French Quarter, where the traditions of an ancient people are duly honored, three slightly troublesome spirits remain comfortably ensconced. Angelique, Joseph, and Mary are confident that the Gaelic greeting posted on the door, *Céad Mile Fáilte*, A Thousand Welcomes!, is meant expressly for them.

19

Ghosts with a Four-Star Rating

The inhabitants of the Big Easy have steadfastly placed a high priority on the pursuit of pleasure. *Laissez les bons temps rouler.* A few resolute souls extended the "let the good times roll" mandate well beyond the confines of life. Theirs was a love affair of the palate—a fondness for fine dining. Not willing to forgo their single-minded quest for Epicurean delights, these spirits make their reservations early and often at one of New Orleans' preeminent dining establishments: Arnaud's restaurant in the French Quarter.

Waiters emerge from the kitchen, bowing under trays laden with appetizers of *Shrimp Arnaud,* swimming in a tangy Creole rémoulade sauce, and *Oysters Bienville.* Steaming plates of *Speckled Trout Meunière,* deep fried and succulent, and *Petit Filet Lafitte* are positioned carefully on crisp, snow-white tablecloths. An intoxicating brew of flaming café brûlot mingles with the sweet aroma of heavenly dessert treats: *Crème Brûlée* and *Chocolate Devastation*—seductive selections guaranteed to tempt the discriminating diner, whether he resides in this world or the next.

Wrapped in this heady atmosphere, guests in the main dining room are seldom aware their every move is being scrutinized by a highly critical apparition. Formally dressed in a turn-of-the-century tuxedo, he stands with his back to the immense paneled windows spanning the front of the restaurant. The headlights of passing cars on Bienville Street pierce the beveled glass, splaying fragments of amber light across the black-and-white mosaic tile floor. Irritated by the intrusion of the outside world into his private domain, the ghost waves his arms in an attempt to block the glare of the offending lights. Engrossed in savoring their gourmet meals, the diners seldom look up.

The tuxedo-clad ghost, however, has just begun his nightly inspection: he notes a smudge on a crystal wineglass; a wilted petal on a yellow rose poised artfully in a bud vase merits a raised eyebrow; improperly folded napkins induce a slight frown. But the ghost's most menacing looks are reserved for the presentation of the food. An errant drip of rémoulade sauce on the edge of a plate or pompano served with a less-than-generous dollop of crabmeat evoke a ferocious scowl from the all-too-observant ghost. Startled busboys have been known to drop entire serving trays, sending silverware and broken bits of china skidding across the floor. The clamor is enough to penetrate the satiated haze enveloping the diners, but they are at a loss to see what has triggered the busboys' clumsy actions. The disgusted ghost has vanished.

Longtime staff know he will be back and, after a short break to compose himself, will likely reappear on the balcony overlooking the main dining room. The restaurant is his kingdom, and despite these few minor lapses, he is justifiably proud of its four-star rating. Most evenings find the spirited "Count" beaming at present owner Archie Casbarian's impeccable guardianship of Arnaud's restaurant.

The ghost is none other than the dashing Count Arnaud Cazenave, founder of the grand restaurant that bears his name. Born in 1876 in the French village of Bosdarros, this former wine salesman embarked on his life's passion—creating a restaurant that would embody his philosophy of dining. In 1920, Count Arnaud set out to transform New Orleans into the "Paris of America," particularly in all matters culinary. To the self-appointed count (he simply appropriated the title) it was vital to remember that eating was not a means to an end. His guiding principles remain emblazoned on back of the restaurant's menu: "A dinner chosen according to one's needs, tastes, and moods, well prepared and well served, is a joy to all senses and a compelling incentive to sound sleep, good health and long life." In short, fine dining offered the cure for life's woes.

Death proved no deterrent to this man on a mission to elevate the pleasures of the table to an art form. Count Arnaud Cazenave died a month short of his seventy-second birthday in 1948, but has never completely relinquished the reins to his signature restaurant. His surprise "quality-control" inspections keep the staff alert. His jarring appearances, where he fades in and out at will, are reminders (especially to new wait staff) that Arnaud's standards of excellence are "second to none."

If the Count's proprietary manifestations are not enough, his imposing portrait, flanked on either side by matching portraits of his two favorite women, hangs over the tables in the main dining room like the icon of a patron saint. The display provides a curious insight into this colorful character. The trio of mammoth portraits is a compelling vision of a charming gentleman about to step forth from his gilded frame and offer his arms to escort the ladies to their table. A prevailing rumor hints that the Count never quite made up his mind, dallying between his wife, the Lady Irma, and her sister, Marie Lamothe. In fact, his entire operation was designed for intrigue.

From the restaurant's inception, Arnaud Cazenave intended to create a sumptuous retreat where one could "throw all cares to the wind, relax completely, and dine leisurely and well." Pleasure-loving New Orleanians embraced the affable Count and his emphasis on a carefree society.

Arnaud's concept proved so popular that he quickly expanded. Buying up one adjoining building after another, the Count soon had, sprinkled throughout a baker's dozen of assorted dwellings, private dining rooms catering to the special needs of his clientele.

Like elsewhere in the tightly packed confines of the French Quarter, where the walls of one dwelling butt hips with the next in forced kinship, each building wrests its fashionable independence from its neighbors with gaily painted bricks, balconies, overhangs, and trims. Arnaud Cazenave cleverly retained this illusion of separate dwellings.

From the exterior, his thirteen buildings resemble a "Mad Hatter's Tea Party" of mismatched architectural elements. A shocking pink Creole cottage squats next to two jaunty townhouses—one a glorious lemon yellow with ribbons of blue trim, the other a delicate flesh-toned tan framed with aquamarine louvered shutters. The Bienville Street lineup includes a large raspberry-red 1838 mansion, home to the original Arnaud's restaurant. This central building is dominated by a gallery and covered balcony packaged in iron grillwork of leprechaun green. The main entrance is marked by a black-and-white tile mosaic bearing Arnaud's distinctive signature script. Holding sway at the corner of Bienville and Bourbon is another pink Creole cottage, this one glowing with brilliant turquoise shutters; its slightly more sedate neighbor is dressed in yellow, with highlights of white and mauve blue.

Only the very astute might discern the common thread in these colorfully costumed structures encompassing three-quarters of a city block. They are all linked by a series of serpentine passageways and secret corridors—the better to serve the discreet comings and goings of Arnaud's privileged clientele. The second- and third-floor private dining chambers seat a romantic tryst for two to a party of two hundred intimate friends and acquaintances. From the palatial Count's Room to the delicate Dauphine Room, from Irma's Room to the gaudy Gold Room, each has a distinct ambiance—and a private entrance. Arnaud's current marketing materials boast that the buzzers to summon waiters to the locked rooms are kept in working order.

During the Count's heyday, many Creole gentlemen and ladies took full advantage of the restaurant's reputation for absolute discretion. The numerous exits and entrances from one building to the next facilitated many a clandestine meeting, much to the delight of the magnanimous Count, who amassed a fortune in money, and favors owed.

Hiding in the inky depths of angled turns, a pair of eyes sneak a furtive look, then quickly cast away. The soft rustle of a satin ball gown, a discreet cough, a glint from a diamond ring, a glimpse of a white boutonnière, the perfumed scent of jasmine, the smoky curl from a cigar—subtle hints abound—haunting remnants, reminders that a few of the Count's favored friends linger on in this pleasure palace of refined taste.

Arnaud's is still the only restaurant that must deploy a small army of waiters just to help guests find their way to their tables. Like traffic cops stationed at strategic intersections, they direct diners through narrow passages, snaking up, then down again, while winding circuitously through the network of buildings. Such measures are a necessity, as it is easy to get lost just on a trip to the bathroom. Caught in the baffling maze of locked doors, multileveled hallways, and odd floor plans, a guest could easily travel half a city block from his/her table, and never have left the restaurant.

On his deathbed, the Count bequeathed the management of his beloved establishment to a designated kindred spirit, his daughter, Germaine Cazenave Wells. Loud, lusty, and prone to dramatic episodes, Germaine is the most likely candidate for the second ghost haunting Arnaud's restaurant.

Although waiter Ron Waldridge had heard tales of ghostly guests unwilling to relinquish their choice tables, he did not believe in hauntings until he bumped into a mysterious lady floating several inches off the floor. Ron, a quiet young man not prone to storytelling, was coming to the end of a typically hectic shift. "I was in the Richelieu Dining Room. I was very busy, and as I looked down the dining room I saw . . ." Here Ron hesitates, unwilling even now to acknowledge the memory of the phantom that confronted him. Staring down at his feet, he draws a deep breath before continuing. "I saw—it was an apparition of a woman. I saw her from a profile and she moved slowly above the floor, across the hallway, and kinda passed into the other wall. She was wearing a big floppy hat and kind of a blouse with puffy sleeves." Sweat pops out on the pale forehead of the shy waiter. "I was kind of shaken." A short self-deprecating laugh punctuates his speech. "I really didn't know what to do, so at first I kept my mouth shut, but I really wanted to go home." Looking up for the first time, Ron is emphatic. "That's what I saw."

A female co-worker on duty with Ron confirms that something traumatic occurred. "I didn't see what he saw. I just ran into him right after it happened. Whatever it was shook him up a whole lot. He didn't want to talk about it. He even had to sit down for a few minutes before he could go back to work."

Ron's description of the female ghost is sketchy, but it does provide one telltale detail—the wide-brimmed hat. Germaine Cazenave Wells was inordinately fond of extravagant finery; elaborate *chapeaux* were a crowning passion. She believed that the fine art of "ogling" in New Orleans needed a little boost, and she was just the one to provide the necessary pizzazz. To cap off a lifetime of strutting her stuff, Germaine decided it was high time New Orleans had a full-blown Easter parade. The attention-grabbing lady gathered together a few of her closest cronies and led a retinue of horse-drawn buggies from Arnaud's restaurant to St. Louis Cathedral on Easter Sunday. Swathed in layers of pastel tulle, necks dripping with strands of pearls and heads adorned with eye-popping Easter bonnets, Germaine's ladies gave the holiday crowd a grand reason to ogle.

If a bonnet-wearing ghost chose to stroll in front of the hapless Ron Waldridge at Arnaud's, it could have been none other than the headstrong Germaine Wells. Given her love of the limelight, it is impossible to imagine she would allow any other female spirit to garner all the attention.

During her lifetime, Germaine opened the original Carnival Memory Room at Arnaud's restaurant on September 15, 1952. To ensure her place in New Orleans fabled history, the tableaus in this room eulogize her crowning achievements;

Germaine reigned as queen of more Mardi Gras royal courts than any individual in Carnival. For the uninitiated, Carnival royalty in New Orleans are selected by the various private krewes or clubs that sponsor the masked balls and parades enjoyed by the masses. Their brief reign usually extends from Twelfth Night to Mardi Gras Day. Germaine maneuvered, manipulated, and cajoled her way into being addressed as "Her Majesty" for a record-breaking thirty-one years, from 1937 to 1968. After all, if her father was "*The* Count" (sans any actual noble pedigree), then Germaine would be *The* Queen, reigning over some twenty-two Mardi Gras balls.

In 1983 present owner Archie A. Casbarian restored the exhibit that features many of Germaine's bejeweled and sequined royal robes, costumes, and glittering tiaras. Casbarian chose to reuse the original tableau mannequins to chilling effect. Walking through the stark black hallway is like entering a massive tomb. Germaine clones, impatiently waiting for their call-outs to the dance, are caught in midstep, as if someone has pulled the plug just as the orchestra is about to strike the first note. Frozen smiles and glassy stares are illuminated under flickering ochre-tinted spotlights. And like the languishing Miss Havisham in Dickens' *Great Expectations,* the mannequins are not aging well.

The first tableau on the right, portraying Germaine and her father as the emperor and empress of China in the 1939 Proteus ball, features a mannequin whose index finger dangles precariously from her left hand. Broken at the knuckle, it clings by a thread. The creeping evidence of decay casts a morbid pall, heightening the sense that the past has invaded the present, and at any moment the specter of death will extend its skeletal hand and slam the door, entombing the curious visitor forever in Germaine's eerie world. After all, what's a queen to do without subjects to bow and curtsey to her royal majesty?

Raised by her devoted father as his little princess, Germaine developed a restaurant management style that relied heavily on P.R.—her own. She was often quoted as comparing the restaurant business to high drama. "It's a play in two acts, lunch and dinner." Scandalous rumors about her legendary appetites for alcohol and men were part of the theatrics. Germaine realized early on the value of publicity, and she relished the fame and notoriety she generated for Arnaud's.

Celebrities flocked to this stellar restaurant to see and be seen. Today their autographed photographs, filling countless hallways, are part of the decor. Loretta Young, Errol Flynn, Buffalo Bob, and Howdy Doody share space with the likes of Bob Hope, Kirk Douglas, Dolly Parton, and Bugs Bunny. Immortality is a prized commodity at Arnaud's, yet it perpetuates the sense that *someone* is always watching. The feeling of hundreds of pairs of eyes, even star-studded ones, following a guest's every move is unnerving.

No one is sure whether another formally clad entity, who hovers near the first-floor photo gallery, is a fan of celebrities, but he does keep a running tab at the Richelieu Bar. Connected to the main dining room by a short passageway, this bar is housed in one of Arnaud's oldest buildings, possibly dating to the late 1700s. The dark cavelike paneling is relieved by thick beveled mirrors stretching from the ceiling to the waist-high wainscoting. It is in the mirrors that regular patrons swear they see a ghostly interloper. Perched on a turquoise-covered barstools, savoring Ramon gin fizzes, they look up to see not only their own reflections in the mirror over the bar, but also that of a tall dark gentleman standing over their shoulders. This particular ghost possesses a three-dimensional form, displaying front, rear, and side views. For as the patrons check the mirror in front of them, they also alarmingly get a view of the back of the ghost's head, along with profiles of his patrician nose, full lips, and broad shoulders, from the mirrors around the room.

Determined not to be fooled by some odd refraction of light and glass angles, one "doubting Thomas" stood up and counted the *living* warm bodies enjoying their nightly cocktail in the Richelieu Bar. He then sat back down and counted the human reflections in the mirrors. The numbers didn't tally;

there was one reflection too many. After enlisting the aid of the bartender on duty, requesting he too count the total number of people in the bar, the "doubting Thomas" added up the reflections again. The bartender's total fell one short of the mirrored reflections. The "doubting Thomas" instructed the bartender to pour a drink for the catch-me-if-you-can annoying entity.

Waiter Frank Loftus confirms that the ghost who plays hide and seek has been at it for awhile. "One evening I was locking up and I was passing the Richelieu Bar. I turned around to shut the lights off, and as I looked towards the wall, I saw the figure of a man dressed in a tuxedo. I stopped dead in my tracks. I looked up again, and sure enough this man looked at me and just disappeared through the wall."

Arnaud's Web site states that even their "rock-solid CPA" was rattled when he tried to take inventory in the Richelieu Bar in the predawn hours of New Year's Day. As he was counting bottles, he was greeted by a mass of cold air shot from the end of the bar. Apparently the ghost did not take kindly to having someone look over his shoulder and was attempting to blow him away. The accountant got the chilly message and quickly vacated the premises.

When Count Arnaud embarked on his grand project, there were likely more than a few lost souls swept aside in the process. The thirteen buildings that now comprise Arnaud's restaurant were once in an area designated as "the back of town." Opium dens and "houses of ill repute" flourished in this then less-than-fashionable section of the French Quarter. Making sure Arnaud's stellar standards of excellence prevail, the vigilant spirits of the Count and his daughter, the irrepressible Germaine, continue to screen visitors and monitor the staff.

Count Arnaud Cazenave created a restaurant that was as much about atmosphere and attitude as it was about fine dining. Today the grand aura prevails at Arnaud's restaurant, where a few demanding ghosts occasionally slip in to spice up the meal.

20

The Madam Who Won't Lie Still

They called it Storyville, but fairytales in "The District" were few and far between. In its heyday from 1897 to 1917, vice flourished and prostitution had a place to call home. The reigning madam of New Orleans' red-light district was the flamboyant Josie Arlington. Historian Henri Gandolfo dubbed her "The Prima Donna of Storyville," for she insisted on calling all the shots—right to the end, micromanaging her own funeral. The ghost of Josie Arlington may still be out and about. It seems Madam Josie has some unfinished business near her grave at Metairie Cemetery.

Born Mamie Duebler somewhere around 1864 (a woman never divulges her real age), Josie, called "little Mary," grew up in the Carrollton section of New Orleans. Her conservative, God-fearing parents were certainly distraught when seventeen-year-old Mamie ran away to become the mistress of Philip ("The Schwarz") Lobrano. For the next nine years, gentlemen callers could find this former uptown girl, working under the name Josie Alton, within the darkened rooms of some of New Orleans' most notorious brothels.

Josie was a fiery beauty with a temper to match. Her numerous brawls quickly escalated from name calling to all-out physical assaults. Herbert Asbury, in his 1936 exposé of the tawdry side of the old French Quarter reports, that in one particularly violent 1886 street fight with a "Negro prostitute, Beulah Ripley," Josie lost most of her hair while Beulah "staggered from the scene of combat minus part of her lower lip and half of her ear." Whom or what they were fighting over, time has swept away.

Josie was also fond of reinventing herself. In 1886, tired of having to fork over a share of her earnings, she set up her own shop at 172 Customhouse Street (now Iberville in the Vieux Carré). She called herself Josie Lobrano, but in many ways nothing changed. Her "girls," following their "madam's" lead, were just as contentious; her brothel was the scene of many a bloody "cat fight." Digging into the newspapers and court records of the day, Asbury discovered that Josie's peculiar living arrangements included supporting not only her "fancy man" Schwarz Lobrano, but several members of her family. During the course of one memorable altercation, everyone got in on the act. It ended when Lobrano shot Josie's brother, Peter Duebler. Lobrano was arrested. The first hearing was a fiasco and ended in a mistrial. At his second trial, Philip ("The Schwarz") Lobrano was acquitted, but by then, even the brawling Josie had enough. She kicked everyone out and closed up shop.

The irrepressible Josie next tried a little bait-and-switch tactic to lure a more refined customer. In 1895, an announcement ran in *The Mascot* alerting interested parties to the arrival of a "bona-fide baroness, direct from the Court at St. Petersburg." Said baroness would receive visitors at the "Chateau Lobrano d'Arlington" at the same Customhouse Street address as Josie's old bordello. Josie, reincarnated for the third time as Josie Lobrano d'Arlington, would "facilitate" introductions to the baroness, who preferred to remain incognito and should be addressed as "La Belle Stewart." Gentlemen flocked to Josie's revamped establishment for the opportunity of "meeting" the baroness and a group of other similarly "titled royal ladies." It was an interesting ploy, until the baroness was unveiled as a former sideshow circus performer.

Josie's next go-round was her finest hour in the business. With the money she raked in during the era of the baroness, she went on to build the "grandest and gaudiest" bordello in Storyville.

Prostitution had made inroads into Louisiana almost from the colony's inception. The reigning French monarchs Louis XIV and Louis XV shipped hordes of convicts and prostitutes to their newly acquired territory in hopes of colonizing the vast wasteland. Shortly after the Louisiana Purchase, gamblers, traders, and rough and rowdy keelboatmen descended on the bustling port city of New Orleans. Knowing that the pockets of these arrivals were lined with ready cash, members of the world's oldest profession moved in to service them. New Orleans was fast becoming the wild west of prostitution.

In 1897 a well-meaning alderman (city council member), one Sidney Story, made an exhaustive study to determine how large European cities handled similar dilemmas. Story introduced an ordinance to contain prostitution and prevent houses of ill repute from encroaching into respectable neighborhoods. The Story ordinance decreed: "Be it ordained by the Common Council of the City of New Orleans . . . Section I of Ordinance 13,032 C.S. . . . From and after the first of October, 1897, it shall be unlawful for any prostitute or woman notoriously abandoned to lewdness, to occupy, inhabit, live or sleep in any house, room or closet, situated without the following limits, viz: From the South side of Customhouse Street to the North side of St. Louis Street, and from the lower or wood side of North Basin Street to the lower or wood side of Robertson Street [in the French Quarter]."

The ordinance did not legalize gambling, but sought to contain the "red-light district" to a single area of town, and in the time-honored tradition, only the women were restricted in their movements; no such restraints were put on the men who sought them out. The ordinance was amended in January of 1898 to further make it unlawful outside of this same thirty-eight-block area to "open, operate or carry on any cabaret, concert-saloon or place where *can can* . . . or similar female dancing are shown." The councilman's ordinance created a city within a city where prostitutes could ply their trade safe from the interference of the police. Much to the disgust of the morally upright Sidney Story, the nation's most celebrated red-light district became widely known as "Storyville," a dubious honor he would take to his grave. Storyville came complete with its own Yellow Pages. Dubbed "The Blue Book," it allowed the prospective gentleman caller to "let his fingers do the walking" through a racy assortment of advertisements, illustrations, and hype about "star performers."

The entrepreneurial madam Josie caught on quickly and had already made nice with the political boss of the Fourth Ward (which included Storyville), Thomas C. Anderson. Anderson was a two-term member of the Louisiana legislature, unofficial mayor of the unofficial town of Storyville, and owner of several prosperous bordellos and saloons. Shedding all her previous aliases (Duebler, Alton, Lobrano), Josie now simply called herself Josie Arlington, in honor of Anderson's favorite saloon, the Arlington Annex at the corner of Customhouse and North Basin streets.

Setting up shop in new digs at 215 Basin Street, Josie also christened her fashionable four-story house "The Arlington." Bay windows on three sides, a domed cupola on the roof, intricate gingerbread painted a pristine white—the exterior created the illusion of a chaste Victorian maiden. Inside all such restraints were off. The interior decor erupted into a riot of gilt, purple-velvet drapes, oriental carpets, green-damask chairs and sofas, silver doorknobs, lace curtains, beveled mirrors, cut-glass chandeliers, and bric-a-brac stuffed into every shelf and corner.

Josie's new girls were a far cry from the squabbling unkempt women at her old brothel on Customhouse Street or the fake baroness/sideshow freak of her last scam. At The Arlington, Josie had no fewer than ten "exquisite strumpets," and during Mardi Gras season, the number doubled. The Arlington was the "crème de la crème" of bordellos and Josie Arlington was regarded as "the snootiest madam in America."

With her steady cash flow, the "Snooty Madam" purchased a $35,000 home on Esplanade Avenue, smack in the middle of respectable society. Her shocked female neighbors pointedly ignored her presence. Clearly unimpressed with their disdain, Madam Josie swept by them, smug in the knowledge that she would soon be entertaining their eager husbands in her business establishment on Basin Street.

For the next eight years, Josie Arlington reveled in her role as the "First Lady of Storyville." But in 1905, a fire of unknown origins rocked her world. It caused such severe damage to the interior of The Arlington that Josie was forced to move her girls and set up temporary shop on the second floor of her friend Tom Anderson's saloon. However, the most devastating effect on Josie was psychological. Having narrowly escaped death, she became obsessed with making preparations for her final passing. Unlike most folks, Josie was not concerned for her immortal soul, but rather the disposition of her physical remains. She believed that her final resting place, like her highly touted business establishment and her private mansion on fashionable Esplanade Avenue, must be a lasting monument to her sense of style and a signal to all that little Mamie Duebler had made it on her own.

For more than sixty-five years Henri Gandolfo, historian and scholar par excellence, wrote and lectured on New Orleans' unique Cities of the Dead. The elaborate tombs and cenotaphs spoke volumes to this gifted storyteller. Gandolfo knew every intimate secret, every scandal, every tantalizing bit of gossip about the bodies buried therein. And Gandolfo had the inside scoop on Josie Arlington.

Josie, says Gandolfo, purchased a $2,000 plot in Metairie Cemetery surrounded by the tombs of the social elite of the city. She next summoned Albert Weiblen, the leading builder and designer of tombs, to her Esplanade home. He arrived bearing a portfolio of black and white sketches based on classical tomb designs in Munich, Germany. After a lengthy meeting, Weiblen contracted an Italian artist named Orsini to make a full color drawing of Josie's proposed mausoleum. With the Storyville madam's stamp of approval, Weiblen hired a small army of workers to erect the tomb in record time. As a reward for meeting her deadline, Josie hosted an extravagant champagne supper for the exhausted workmen.

Josie's design choice—almost a self-portrait—was an oddly prophetic one, stirring an epoch of controversy. Carved from highly polished reddish-brown marble from Stonington, Maine, the striking tomb sits on a small grassy mound roped off with a looped chain of cast iron. Two simple pilasters frame the immense double bronze doors of the crypt. These pillars are capped with matching square urns, each holding what some would like to believe are carved renditions of the eternal flame of life. The flip side of this lofty interpretation falls back on the early days of prostitution in New Orleans. Flambeaux, or torches, were lit outside small hovels or cribs on Gallatin Street adjacent to the river to let potential customers know the prostitute was in and open for business. Red lights are a universal symbol for danger and the term "red-light district" is part of the worldwide lexicon—a designated area for vice and prostitution. Josie's urns, with their plumes leaning heavily to the right, give the illusion they have just received a mighty blow from a hefty gust of wind off the river.

If Josie selected these symbolic torches to represent her chosen profession, or they were simply part of Weiblen's concept, we will never know. But these are minor touches compared to the life-size bronze statue of a woman standing just outside the tomb.

The controversial statue was created by German sculptor F. Bagdon in 1911. Artfully draped in a flowing Grecian gown, the voluptuous full figure commands attention. The statue's right foot is poised just inches from the door, while the left leg is one step down. In her left arm, the female statue holds a bouquet of roses, but it is her right arm that generates the most gossip. Reaching forward, her fingertips almost, but not quite, touch the door. "See," say sympathetic insiders, "it's poor Josie locked out again by her heartless father. She's stuck outside, banging on the door trying to get back in!" Those who live near Metairie Cemetery swear the statue of the maiden comes back to life "angrily pounding the slab with both metallic fists with a din that may be heard for blocks."

Support for the rationale behind the compelling statue is captured in *Gumbo Ya-Ya*, a delightful collection of some of Louisiana's most popular folktales. Editors Lyle Saxon, Edward Dreyer, and Robert Tallant believe that Josie's troubles can all be heaped on dear old Dad: seventeen-year-old Josie (Mamie Duebler) did not run away at all. Like most teenage girls, she stayed out beyond curfew one evening and her father locked her out. Ignoring his daughter's anguished pleas, the stubborn Mr. Duebler refused to let her back in. Vowing that no one would ever slam a door in her face again, young Mamie embarked on a career that would ensure her financial independence. Josie (the former Mamie) would now and forever be in control of her own destiny.

This same terror of being locked out in life carried over to Josie's careful preparations for her final resting place. It would be the ultimate irony if Josie Arlington was condemned to pounding for admittance to her own grave.

This interpretation is rejected by the self-righteous who prefer to think that the statue is actually an apt representation of "Josie, The Scarlet Harlot, knocking in vain at the gates of heaven."

All sides overlook the facts: Josie Arlington personally selected every detail of her own memorial, making sure there would always be a place for her; Madam Arlington would have no desire to see herself depicted ad infinitum as a helpless young girl denied admittance by a cruel papa, or banned at the pearly gates by a stern archangel.

A closer look at the bronze figure reveals no signs of distress: her face is serene; her fingers are relaxed; she is neither pulling on the large ringed doorknockers nor pounding with her fists. This is a self-assured, sensuous woman returning from a stroll in the garden, eager to fill the interior of her lasting abode with the aroma of freshly picked flowers.

A much-quoted tale, first published in 1945 in *Gumbo Ya-Ya: Folk Tales of Louisiana,* unequivocally states, "Twice the Maiden has taken walks." At night the statue turns, travels down the five granite steps, and meanders about the grounds. The ghost of Josie making house calls? Josie looking up old friends?

In *Metairie Cemetery—An Historical Memoir,* author Henri Gandolfo reveals one final tidbit about Miss Josie Arlington. It seems that the Storyville madam who spent her life in the company of men never intended to sleep alone for all eternity; Josie specifically instructed builder Weiblen to expand the original design to accommodate two burial vaults. The unnamed intended co-occupant never had a chance to move in.

In spite of Josie's well-laid plans, her funeral and its aftermath were a fiasco. Josie died on February 14, 1914, three years after the completion of her tomb. She was at best estimates fifty years old. While the grave was awash with flowers from anonymous "benefactors," the service was sparsely attended: Tom Anderson, the "mayor" of Storyville, John T. Brady, her personal manager, a civil court judge, and a priest.

That evening, with Josie's body barely settled in, a passerby was awestruck by the phenomenon blazing before him. The two granite flambeaux atop the columns on the Storyville madam's tomb were flickering a brilliant red. Crowds gathered to witness the spectacle. "Look—Josie's open for business!" they shouted. Night after night curious hordes of people, convinced that Josie had set up shop and was accepting callers in the afterlife, converged on the shell road running alongside the cemetery. Historian Gandolfo comments sardonically that "entertainment must have been hard to come by in those days." To maintain order, police detachments had to remain on duty all night.

Metairie Cemetery officials were mortified by this unseemly

state of affairs and scrambled to find a way to halt it. Finally one astute cemetery worker noticed a recently installed light at the toll barrier of the nearby New Basin Shell Road. As the beacon swung in the breeze, its beam bounced off the polished granite of Josie's tomb. Gandolfo notes that while the reflection of the beacon did spill over to other nearby tombs, "it was only the Duebler [Arlington] tomb that provided the supernatural display" of flashing light. An order was quickly given to plant a massive line of shrubs as a barrier between the outside row of tombs in the cemetery and the toll beacon. A large cross was also etched on the rear of the tomb—a little Christian grisgris to deflect the devil's work. Neither the shrubs nor the cross had any impact. Josie's tomb continued to send out its scandalous signal.

Finally, after a little negotiation with the proprietors of the toll road, the signal light was extinguished completely, effectively pulling the plug on the nocturnal display. The crowds dispersed and Josie should have been able to rest easier.

A new wrinkle arrived in the form of Josie's convent-raised niece. Following in the footsteps of her "Aunt Mamie," the young niece became enamored with her own "fancy man," John Brady, Josie's close friend and former business manager. In her will, Josie bequeathed her considerable assets to her niece and John, knowing nothing of their clandestine affair. The pair squandered their inheritance in an astonishingly short period of time, even by fun-loving New Orleans' standards. The financially strapped couple sold off Josie's magnificent private mansion on Esplanade Avenue, and when that wasn't enough, the tomb was next on the auction block!

In the only-in-New Orleans category, a prominent family purchased the tomb of the Storyville madam, naively believing that the prostitute's notoriety would magically disappear once they had their name carved in large block letters over the doors of the crypt. "Foolish mortals," the spirit of Josie chuckled. "There is nothing so enduring as a good scandal."

Naturally, before any dearly departed relative of the new

owners was interred in Josie's tomb, Josie had to go. It must have been quite a sight to see workmen in the dead of night pull open the heavy bronze doors, lift the displaced madam, and whisk her body to an undisclosed location.

As gruesome as this might sound, moving bodies about is standard operating procedure in New Orleans—a burial custom practiced in the city up to and including the present day. Bernard ("Irv") Zoller of Lake Lawn Metairie Cemeteries explains: "It's called the year-and-a-day rule. Anytime after one year has passed, a burial can be disturbed. The casket is taken out of the vault; the remains are taken out of the casket and put into another container, which is today a small plastic pouch, like a small body bag. The casket is destroyed."

Zoller casually goes on to list several options available for the disposition of the bagged remains. "Cemetery workers, at the request of the family, will put the pouch . . . on a shelf in the back of the vault, in the lower recesses of the vault" (a small basement, if you will). "If there is space," says Zoller, the remains of the displaced family member are returned and placed "on top of the new casket." Zoller adds one final option to this list of disposal selections. "They've even put them inside the casket, if it's a spouse that's being buried." Family togetherness carried to the extreme—the new corpse gets to cradle the bagged remains of his/her previously deceased loved one.

In Josie's case none of the above was a viable alternative. The new tomb owners had no inclination to share. And given Miss Arlington's propensity to attract attention (both in life and death), cemetery officials were not about to risk a repeat performance. Josie's new burial site is, according to Henri Gandolfo, "one of Metairie Cemetery's most closely guarded secrets."

Just to the left of the original gates of the old cemetery is a white stucco, red-tiled-roof building resembling a Spanish-style church complete with bell tower. No worship services are conducted within—this is the "Receiving Vault"; it holds the bodies of those with nowhere else to go.

Many of Metairie's grandiose tombs were not finished in time. Bodies were placed in a holding pattern inside the "Receiving Vault" until the intended tomb was complete, or, in the case of someone like Josie, a body was stored here until other arrangements were made. A present-day cemetery worker, who prefers his anonymity, asserts that "numerous unclaimed bodies are stacked inside."

If Josie's body was secretly stashed here, rest assured Madam's spirit would never take such matters lying down, and her story may still have a happy ending. A charming encounter involving the spirit of Josie and a famous hero was shared with producer Barbara Sillery during the making of *The Haunting of Louisiana*.

Each year at Halloween the Friends of the Cabildo, in support of the Louisiana State Museum, host a weekend "Ghostly Galavant" through the French Quarter. Costumed docents take on the roles of legendary New Orleans characters. On one such weekend, a slightly tipsy older woman gave her character, Josie Arlington, free rein. Regaling the tour crowded into a private courtyard with tales of her bawdy escapades at various brothels, the actress "Josie" boasted they all came to her: governors, mayors, statesmen, generals—society's finest. The docent wrapped up her performance by telling the amazing story of her burial vault. After receiving some polite clapping, the exhausted "Josie" sank onto a concrete bench. Producer Barbara Sillery leaned over to congratulate the docent on her entertaining portrayal. Looking up through watery-blue eyes, "Josie" whispered: "You know, they think it's so sad I was kicked out of my tomb and stuck somewhere else. We're having the best time."

Intrigued, Sillery asked, "We?"

"Yes," replied the rejuvenated "Josie." "Toussy and I have a lot to talk about now."

"And by Toussy you mean?" prompted Sillery.

"Why, Gen. Pierre Gustave Toutant Beauregard, of course!"

In life, the irreverent Josie was eminently the type to flirt with a handsome Confederate hero. Josie was in her prime when Beauregard returned to New Orleans after the war. When the general died at the age of seventy-five, his solemn funeral and burial in Metairie Cemetery left a lasting impression on the Storyville madam. His body was interred in the tumulus (a burial chamber built into an earthen mound) of the Benevolent Association, Army of Tennessee, Louisiana Division. By a formal act of the association, Beauregard's remains can never be removed. The slab over his crypt carries an eternal guarantee—sort of a perpetual Do Not Disturb sign.

Although she chose to be buried close by in Metairie Cemetery, the unlucky Josie, unlike the general, has a hard time staying put. Her body may have been tossed into the "Receiving Vault," but her spirit refuses to be contained. The lingering ghost of the Storyville madam seems well suited to inhabit the beautiful female form at her former tomb. And if the statue occasionally steps down for a short walk to reminisce with an old friend, could this not simply be Josie, once again taking charge? A desire to beat the odds is a powerful force.

So for Josie Arlington, wherever she may lie, a lasting epitaph:

She played all the angles; her life and death
remain glittering beacons in New Orleans' storied past.

Epilogue

"Things that go bump in the night" are rooted deep in Louisiana's ethnically diverse folk-life and storytelling traditions. Like the meandering Ol' Man River that defines it, Louisiana and her people follow their own ethereal rhythms, patterns, and beliefs. Their affinity and affection for home-grown ghosts continue to generate a lively debate.

Anne Fitzgerald, owner of Loyd Hall: "It's just a part of life and part of what goes on here. We're Southerners and people tend to think that in the Deep South we're kind of crazy at times anyway. Maybe it's just the heat and humidity and overactive imaginations, but when you live in a structure such as this you have to accept the ghosts and spirits that are here, just as you accept the fact that you don't have central heat and air. Ghosts are all part of what goes to make this house a home."

Retired Catholic archbishop Philip M. Hannan: "They say all this stuff about haunted houses. This is nonsense. It's a game; it's just a pastime. I think it has bad overtones because it entices people to get into that kind of thing and can lead them to devil worship."

Mary Louise Prudhomme, director of the Old State Capitol

Museum: "Do I think ghosts and hauntings are possible? Don't you? I think anything's possible. Yes, I believe; there's too many things that have happened here to make me know that someone else made that possible that was not associated in the physical form. I believe that, but I don't study it. I don't lay awake at night worrying about it. I just think you have to be open to the possibilities."

Fr. William Maestri, Catholic moral theologian: "Ghosts, spirits of the dead, can't just pop in and out, like on some divine escalator."

Edith Layton, Ormond Plantation: "Just because we can't see something does not mean it does not exist. So perhaps ghosts are on a different plane of existence. It would be nice to think that when we go from this body that we've had for our whole life, we go to another plane and that all the knowledge we have amassed is not lost."

Archbishop E. J. Johnson, Israelite Divine Black Spiritual Church: "It's all in the mind. If you pray hard enough you can communicate with spirits and there are times you can see them . . . you got earthbound spirits and you got heavenbound spirits. The good spirit will help you and the bad spirit will get you in trouble . . . if you pray and the Holy Ghost takes you, you can talk in Italian, Japanese, or whatever kind of spirit takes you that's what you talk in; they just take control of your body and your voice and they talk in their voice. All this is mystery stuff and a lot of people don't understand it and you can't understand it unless you pray for wisdom and knowledge."

Father Maestri: "There are so many people who are afraid of ghosts and afraid of spirits . . . I don't think it's the dead that we need to be afraid of, I think it's the living. The best thing we can do for the dead is to love them while they're living."

Maida Owens, director of the Louisiana Folklife Program: "I think things are changing concerning beliefs in the supernatural. In the past, ghosts were considered malevolent. They were something to be scared of. But more recently it seems a spirit is less likely to be seen as something that would harm as something that's coming to a friendly visit. I think all of us want to have some kind of assurance about what's going to happen after death. Personally I find it [the possibility of returning spirits] comforting and it doesn't scare me at all . . . during my mother's funeral a friend told me later that the chandeliers suddenly started spinning slightly at one point and it was during the time where one family member was speaking. Then as that person stopped, the chandelier stopped. Now I would like to believe that this is my mother showing approval, letting us know that she liked what she was hearing rather than my mother haunting us or showing disapproval. So I think that's sort of an example of how personal belief systems can determine how we approach these things, whether or not it's a scary ghost or a sweet visit."

Scary or sweet, the haunted label is permanently affixed to *La Belle Dame Créole*.

Orleans criminal sheriff Charles Foti: "We have a richer heritage [in New Orleans]. It's like a gumbo. It is like a mixing together of the French and the Spanish and the Italians and the Irish and the African-Americans—everybody together. You make this roux and this gumbo comes out of it and it's rich and it's tasty and it's good and it's earthy, and I think that's what we have that other people don't have."

Father Maestri: "What you have here is all of these influences—cultural, religious, social—and the way they exist in Louisiana is that we take fragments and say, 'Yes, I like that, that fits in here; ooh, I think I like a little of that!' We have become kind of cultural and religious bag ladies. We hate to throw things away. And so instead we claim them as our own, put them in a form we recognize, and it helps us to coexist."

New Orleans physic "Taz": "You've got a place that mixed in with legends of Marie Laveau . . . there's an aura of mysticism in New Orleans. People come to relax and be themselves. Some of them become kids and allow themselves to believe in spirits, because here it is not looked at as being odd—at that point you become one of the normal people here."

Director Mary Louise Prudhomme: "You could almost put a fence around Louisiana because it's so different from the rest of the United States. Ghosts, politicians, food, you name it—in those areas we're unique."

Those living in the mystical kingdom of *La Louisiane* are not likely to relinquish their love affair with the past anytime soon. As for this author, I remain enthralled. Ghosts, apparitions, spirits have a very real presence here. It is impossible to sit across from Ruth Bodenheimer in the parlor of the Lanaux Mansion and not be aware of the influence of her in-house decorator, Mr. Charles Andrew Johnson. It is unnerving to look into the face of waiter Ron Waldridge at Arnaud's restaurant and wonder what he has seen. And it is magical to wander the grounds of Loyd Hall at night, to peer into bedrooms, to stand on the balcony and imagine that maybe, just maybe, I hear the mournful Harry Henry pulling the bow across the strings of his violin.

I take comfort in the wise counsel of Father Maestri: "We are told by our culture that the only thing that matters is science, which you can taste, see, touch, smell, measure. That's reality. Well, there is something in the human spirit that rebels against that . . . there's whole levels and dimensions of life that are simply going to come out whether we like it or not."

Here in Louisiana we like it very much indeed.

Appendix
Selected Haunted Sites

Plantations

Chretien Point Plantation
665 Chretien Point Rd.
Sunset, LA 70584
(337) 662-5876
Open for daily tours and bed and breakfast

Destrehan Plantation
13034 River Rd.
Destrehan, LA 70047
(504) 764-9315
Open for daily tours

Loyd Hall
292 Loyd Bridge Rd.
Cheneyville, LA 71325
(318) 776-5641
Open for tours and bed and breakfast

Madewood Plantation
4250 Hwy. 308
Napoleonville, LA 70390
(504) 369-7151
Open for tours and bed and breakfast

Oak Alley Plantation
3645 Hwy. 18
Vacherie, LA 70090
(225) 265-2151
Open for daily tours and overnight accommodations

Ormond Plantation
13786 River Rd.
Destrehan, LA 70047
(504) 764-8544
Open for daily tours and overnight accommodations

The Myrtles
Highway 61
St. Francisville, LA 70775
(225) 635-6277
Open for tours and overnight accommodations

Woodland Plantation
21997 Hwy. 23
West Point a La Hache, LA 70083
(800) 231-1514
Open for tours and overnight accommodations

Hotels/Bed and Breakfasts

Lafitte's Guest House
1003 Bourbon St.
New Orleans, LA 70130
(504) 581-2678

The Lanaux Mansion
547 Esplanade Ave.
New Orleans, La 70116
(800) 729-4640

Museums

The Beauregard-Keyes House
1113 Chartres St.
New Orleans, LA 70116
(504) 523-7257
Open for daily tours

The Old State Capitol
100 North Blvd.
Baton Rouge, LA 70801
(800) 488-2968
Open for tours

Restaurants/Music Clubs

Arnaud's
813 Rue Bienville
New Orleans, LA 70112
(504) 523-5433

Lafitte's Blacksmith Shop and Bar
941 Bourbon St.
New Orleans, LA 70130
(504) 523-0066

O'Flaherty's Irish Channel Pub
514 Toulouse St.
New Orleans, LA 70130
(504) 529-1317

Tours

Chacahoula Bayou Tours
492 Louisiana St.
Westwego, LA 70094
(504) 436-2640

Videos

*The Haunting of Louisiana
Plantation Portraits*
Keepsake Productions, Inc.
25 Kings Canyon Dr.
New Orleans, LA 70131
e-mail: bsillery@home.com
VHS copies: The Louisiana Catalog
(800) 375-4100 www.lacat.com

Selected Bibliography

Arthur, Stanley Clisby. *Old New Orleans: Walking Tours of the French Quarter.* Gretna, La.: Pelican Publishing Company, 1995.

Asbury, Herbert. *The French Quarter: An Informal History of the New Orleans Underworld.* New York: Alfred A. Knopf, 1936.

Baudier, Roger. *The Catholic Church in Louisiana.* New Orleans: The Archdiocese of New Orleans, 1939.

Bodin, Ron. *Voodoo Past and Present.* Lafayette, La.: The Center for Louisiana Studies, University of Southwestern Louisiana, 1990.

Bultman, Bethany Ewald. *New Orleans.* New York: Fodor's Travel Publications, 1998.

Chase, John. *Frenchmen, Desire, Good Children . . . and Other Streets of New Orleans!* Gretna, La.: Pelican Publishing Company, 2001.

Cowan, Walter G., Charles L. Dufour, John C. Chase, O. K. LeBlanc, and John Wilds. *New Orleans Yesterday and Today.* Baton Rouge: Louisiana State University Press, 1983.

Cummings, Light Townsend, Joe Gray Taylor, William Ivy Hair, Mark T. Carleton, and Michael L. Kurtz. *Louisiana: A History.* Edited by Bennet H. Wall. Wheeling, Ill.: Forum Press, 1984.

Danaher, Kevin. *The Year in Ireland.* Dublin: Mercier Press, 1972.

DeHart, Jess. *Plantations of Louisiana.* Gretna, La.: Pelican Publishing Company, 2001.

Dobie, J. Frank. "The Mystery of Lafitte's Treasure." *The Yale Review* 18 (September 1928).

Dufour, Charles L. *Ten Flags in the Wind: The Story of Louisiana.* New York: Harper and Row, 1967.

Florence, Robert. *City of the Dead: A Journey Through St. Louis Cemetery #1.* Lafayette, La.: The Center for Louisiana Studies, University of Southwestern Louisiana, 1996.

———. *New Orleans Cemeteries: Life in the Cities of the Dead.* New Orleans: Batture Press, 1997.

Fry, Gladys-Marie. *Night Riders in Black Folk History.* Athens, Ga.: Brown Thrasher Books, 1991.

Gandolfo, Henri A. *Metairie Cemetery: An Historical Memoir, Tales of Its Great Statesmen, Soldiers and Great Families.* Metairie, La.: Stewart Enterprises, 1981.

Gehman, Mary. *The Free People of Color of New Orleans: An Introduction.* New Orleans: Margaret Media, 1994.

Heard, Malcolm. *French Quarter Manual: An Architectural Guide to New Orleans' Vieux Carré.* Jackson, Miss.: University Press of Mississippi, 1997.

Huber, Leonard V. *New Orleans: A Pictorial History.* Gretna, La.: Pelican Publishing Company, 1991.

——— and Samuel Wilson, Jr. *The Basilica on Jackson Square: The History of St. Louis Cathedral and Its Predecessors.* New Orleans: St. Louis Cathedral, 1965.

Johnson, Jerah. *Congo Square in New Orleans.* New Orleans: The Louisiana Landmarks Society, 1995.

Kein, Sybil. *Creole: The History and Legacy of Louisiana's Free People of Color.* Baton Rouge: Louisiana State University Press, 2000.

Kemp, John R. *New Orleans: An Illustrated History.* Sun Valley, Calif.: American Historical Press, 1997.

Keyes, Frances Parkinson. *Madame Castel's Lodger.* New York: Farrar, Straus and Company, 1962.

Kniffen, Fred B., Hiram F. Gregory, and George A. Stokes. *The Historic Indian Tribes of Louisiana.* Baton Rouge: Louisiana State University Press, 1987.

Le Gardeur, Rene J., Jr., Samuel Wilson, Allen Begnaud, Gilbert Gurbin, Robert L. Allain, F. A. Graugnard, Charles Hodson, and Harold S. Birkett. *Green Fields: Two Hundred Years of Louisiana Sugar.* Lafayette, La.: The Center for Louisiana Studies, University of Southwestern Louisiana, 1980.

McCarthy, Ann. *The Mississippi River.* Surrey, U.K.: Colour Library Books, 1987.

Martinez, Raymond J. *Marie Laveau, Voodoo Queen.* Gretna, La.: Pelican Publishing Company, 2001.

—— and Jack D. L. Holmes. *New Orleans Facts and Legends.* Jefferson, La.: Hope Publications, n.d.

Saxon, Lyle. *Fabulous New Orleans.* Gretna, La.: Pelican Publishing Company, 1988.

——, Edward Dreyer, and Robert Tallant. *Gumbo Ya-Ya: Folk Tales of Louisiana.* Gretna, La.: Pelican Publishing Company, 1987.

——. *Lafitte the Pirate.* Gretna, La.: Pelican Publishing Company, 1989.

Taylor, Joe Gray. *Louisiana: A Bicentennial History.* New York: W. W. Norton & Company, 1976.

Toledano, Roulhac B. *The National Trust Guide to New Orleans: The Definitive Guide to Architectural and Cultural Treasures.* New York: John Wiley & Sons, 1996.

Twain, Mark. *Life on the Mississippi.* New York: The Modern Library, 1993.